Passion for Freedom

Passion
for Freedom

Maria's Story

by Maria Gomori

Science and Behavior Books, Inc.
PALO ALTO, CALIFORNIA

Printed in the United States of America.

Library of Congress Card Number 2001 131034
ISBN 0-8314-0090-0

Cover design by Jim Marin/Marin Graphics
Editing, interior design, and typesetting by Rain Blockley
Printing by Banta Book Group

Contents

I dedicate this book to my
family—
my late husband Paul, my
son Andy, and
my grandsons Paul and
Steve

Foreword

In this era of mass production of books and movies, why should we be interested in yet another autobiography? The answer is because we have much to learn about the structure of human nature. Most people succumb to the ravages of their lives, becoming the quintessential victims of time and circumstances. It is a common belief that history determines a person's destiny. In most instances, we would agree. However, we are aware of some people who appear to rise beyond their circumstances to shape history itself, rather than to be shaped by it. Their stories are the stuff of heroism, courage, and inspiration. Such is the case of Maria Gomori.

While the twentieth century may be seen as the century of discovery and rapid growth, the ensuing millennium appears to be embarking on a dangerous course of "rights," expectations, and entitlements. Rather than supporting the avowed aims of equality for all, such philosophies and legislation may be eroding efforts that stem from attempts to assuage guilt rather than from the resonance of a more caring and understanding nature. Perhaps by carefully examining the lives of more autonomous individuals, such as Maria Gomori, we will gain some insights that will inspire us to work toward healthier and more fulfilling choices in our own lives.

Premonitions of a future life of distinction could be seen in the child Maria. She was raised in the intellectually vibrant atmosphere of early twentieth century Hungary. Her father in particular saw her high intelligence and stimulated her love of learning. She was steeped in the classical arts as a youngster. But she early on showed the signs of rebelliousness that in later life would mellow into the staunchly principled approach to her life. When she was sent to the opera on Saturday afternoons, she secreted a copy of Dostoevsky with her so that she could continue to study while she did her duty to the arts.

In the tumultuous times of World War II, she did not succumb to the temptations of bitterness and resignation. Instead, she continued to fight the oppression, resisting the incursions of aggression by the Nazis and, later, the Russians. She found freedom through her own ingenuity and courage. This is reminiscent of what Eleanor Roosevelt wrote about war's effects. In her introduction to The Diary of a Young Girl, she refers to "war's greatest evil—the degradation of the human spirit." She continues, "At the same time, Anne Frank's diary makes poignantly clear the ultimate shining nobility of that spirit."* Maria's story does the same.

Maria's life is a testimony to the principles addressed by existential philosophies: freedom, authenticity, responsibility, and moral agency. With balance and courage, she also accepts the inevitable challenges of angst, loneliness, and paralysing uncertainties. Her mind is alive with ideas, concepts, and novel perspectives on human beings.

Despite her professional clinical training, she staunchly stuck by her principles of humanism and consideration for the

---

* Frank, Anne (1952). *The Diary of a Young Girl*. Garden City, NY: Doubleday, p. 7.

individual. When she began to teach, she reached in to touch the young, pompous lives of partially trained doctors and social workers. She would never accept dehumanizing objectification—not in a patient, in herself, or in her trainees.

With humor and magnanimity, she drew out the human qualities that were being stifled by the regimentation of depersonalizing training. A generation of professionals has Maria to thank for the warmth and humanity that persist in their practices.

Even though Maria today is a famous expert, she is remarkable in her lifelong pursuit of learning. She does not rest on her laurels; instead, she is always looking for new intellectual wilderness to trek. She is forever questioning, probing, reading and discussing. In all our years of teaching, she is one of the best students we have had. Her questions have taken us further in our own work. Her synthetic abilities are fascinating; she is ever ready to turn things over and find a new approach or attitude. These investigative qualities are admirable in a young person—they are remarkable in an octogenarian! She always has with her a new book or a new idea she is exploring. She is indeed wise and very experienced, yet she approaches her study of life and people with "beginner's mind." She is as eager and keen as we imagine she was in her youthful days at the Sorbonne.

Maria has retained her youthful innocence while amassing considerable wisdom and fortitude. Even to this day, she is a mixture of competence and ingenuousness. Although she is adept at helping others to take charge of their own lives, she is baffled by technology. She is able to deal with the subtleties of family dynamics, and yet she is unsure about changing a light bulb or preparing a complete meal for guests! Although she has spearheaded the development of many professional organizations and training programs, she has a hard time balancing her checkbook without assistance. Nevertheless, she pushes on, laughing at herself and her shortcomings, and never complains or gives up. Her remarkable sense of humor is infectious; her laughter is frequent and engaging.

Her professional career has been marked by innovation, courage, and insightfulness. It has also been punctuated by many awards and honors. She is the author of books and articles about human development, and she has offered workshops around the world to countless people. For many years, she was a special colleague, confidante, and close personal friend of the world-renowned family therapist Virginia Satir. She has become one of the leading international exponents of the Satir model of family therapy, and she has helped to establish Satir centers around the globe. She is a connector, and she prides herself on this.

In Maria's apartment is a photograph of her as a young girl, with her red hair flowing. Even though her chronological age is now advanced, she is still that young girl in spirit. A light of beauty and intelligence glows strong around her. She moves with a youthful vigor that challenges much younger people to keep up. Even today, in her eighty-first year, she is bright and inquisitive. Always, Maria is ready for a new adventure, through the theatre, travels, movies, books, art, music or social gatherings. The numerous rings on her fingers express a dramatic, flamboyant spirit. Her penetrating eyes are warm, accepting, and curious, with no trace of dismissive judgment.

The pages of this book recount a tale of courage. Maria is a singularly remarkable woman—not just because of her amazing personal history of triumph of over dehumanizing forces, but more because of her active engagement with life throughout all her eighty-plus years. Neither ponderous nor negative, she has crafted a living philosophy of positivism in embracing her considerable challenges. She is at once a pragmatist and a prophet, a realist and a dreamer, an inspiration to all who aspire to explore the farther reaches of human nature.

Maria Gomori has never lost her belief in people, much like Anne Frank, whom she admires:

> It's really a wonder that I haven't dropped all my ideals, because they seem so absurd and impossible to carry out. Yet I keep them, because in spite of everything I still believe that people are really good at heart. I simply can't build up my hopes on a foundation consisting of confusion, misery, and death. I see the world gradually being turned into a wilderness, I hear the ever approaching thunder, which will destroy us too, I can feel the sufferings of millions and yet, if I look up into the heavens, I think that it will all come right, that this cruelty too will end, and that peace and tranquillity will return again.*

—Jock McKeen, M.D.
—Bennet Wong, M.D.

Gabriola Island, British Columbia
October 2000

---

* Frank, Anne. *Ibid*, p. 278.

Foreword

As my grandmother, "Babi" has taught me many things throughout my childhood and adult years. A lot of this learning has come through in stories—stories that have been a part of me throughout my entire life. Now, through this book, I'll have a record of these memories in the same voice that I remember them.

As a child, I was drawn to my grandmother though a sense of mystery and excitement. We'd have discussions about the afterlife and some far-off land called Hungary. As an adult, I learned of her many accomplishments and have come to appreciate and understand her more difficult and terrifying times. Her life is inspiring to me and confirms that the roles we play in our lives are driven directly by our own choices.

Babi's story is one of war, love, politics, and passion. It's a story of always looking forward, never back. She is always ready to learn more by meeting and discovering new people; her life is an ongoing learning curve of experience on all levels.

This book is her story, and it shows the strength and the love of life that my grandmother carries with her to this day.

—Paul Gomori

Our situation on this earth seems strange. Everyone appears involuntarily and uninvited for a short stay without knowing why.

—*Albert Einstein*

Preface

In the last few years, I have sometimes told stories of my experiences to a few friends. Many have asked, "Why don't you write a book about your life?" I can talk but I cannot write, so I had given up writing books after co-authoring *The Satir Model*. Then, over lunch in Gabriola during the summer of 1998, Ernie and Cathy McNally offered to turn my stories into this book. That November, I spent three days telling stories in their beautiful house. Wendy Huntington was also there, as well as Graeme Brown. The environment was wonderful, and Graeme audiotaped while Ernie videotaped as I spoke in my Hungarian–English. "I don't know where this is going," I thought, "but at least I'll have a record for my grandchildren about our life." All my life, I have followed the process, letting life unfold as it does; I think I have often survived because I never looked too long at the obstacles. I had faith in my destiny and knew that my intuition and my spirit guides would lead me to the best outcome. So it was with this book. The process evolved step by step.

My old friend Sharon Conrad then offered to do the hard work of transcribing the audiotapes—what turned out to be 300 pages. I decided to go ahead with the book. Soon after, I met Per Brask, who expressed interest in rewriting and rearranging the messy material in the transcript. After talking over the shape and contents of the book and adding more material, we arrived at a draft of these memoirs. He gratefully acknowledges the help Carole Anderson provided him.

My wonderful friend Bob Spitzer expressed interest in publishing the book and told me to send it to his editor, Rain Blockley. I was worried because the first draft was quite unfinished. Rain proceeded miraculously quickly and organized it into this book.

Finally, I thank my son, Andy, for his essential help with the book's photographs and his continued interest, support, and encouragement. I also appreciate my grandsons Paul and Steve for their interest and participation, and our friend Cynthia Wiebe for her helpful comments and participation in the writing of this book. Special thanks to my friend Eleanor Adaskin for her support, patience, and most valued practical and spiritual help.

All these people and my friends added to the reality of this book, and I am very appreciative.

The major purpose is to leave this book to my grandsons and their children. It is easy to forget how we got here, so this will shed some light for them. We came to Canada to live—and to have Andy and his family grow up—in a free country that offers security and respect for humanity. I am grateful. I hope they will remember.

Another purpose is to add to the already available stories about the Holocaust. My stories about the war reflect the horrors and extreme cruelty I witnessed. These experiences are also part of my growing up—as are my many miraculous survivals.

I am amazed when I look back at my life. How did I get to where I am today? How come I am doing what I am doing in Canada and all over the world? I know my curiosity supported me in my learnings and in my being here. During a psychic reading, I was once told that I really did not want to be on this planet this lifetime. I am here only because I was curious about the experience. In a more recent reading, I got the following message: I came unwillingly but did it anyway. That feels okay.

That is the story of much of my life, as this book shows. Often, I experienced life reluctantly; later, when I look back, those times held the greatest learnings for me. One of this book's purposes is to highlight my belief that we can either be the victims of our past or choose to let the past illuminate the present and the future. It's our choice.

Passion for Freedom

In order to be a realist, you
must believe in miracles.

—*David ben Gurion*

What life means to us is
determined not so much by
what life brings to us but
the attitude we bring to life,
not so much by what
happens to us as by our
reaction to what happens.

—*Lewis Dunning*

— 1 —

Shaky Ground

Looking back over my life, I'm very grateful to be alive. One of my more recent life-threatening experiences happened in a London pub in the theater district, where I was eating lunch in the early 1990s. Having bought my discount ticket at Leicester Square for that afternoon's show, and having a few hours in between, I decided to go to one of those nice old pubs, have lunch, and read the paper. I found one and chose a quiet corner in one of its rather large rooms.

Suddenly, I heard an explosion. I didn't know what was happening. (I later found out that a bomb had blown up in the men's washroom, where a man died.) The whole place was a disaster; it looked like a battlefield. Many people were badly injured, but the corner where I was sitting was not damaged at all. I was in total shock, still not really knowing what had happened. As I walked out, I had to step over people's bodies. It was a frightening scene.

Outside were a crowd of people and the police. I realized that I'd left my handbag inside. The police weren't allowing people to go back in, of course. Since my passport and money were in my bag, I had to convince them to let me in. Returning to my table, I saw more of this horrible scene. By the time I got back outside, the police had blocked the whole area, and I was directed to go toward Oxford Street.

I was confused, scared, and in a trance. I wasn't sure whether I was really alive. Perhaps I was in some other place and imagining that I was still in London, walking along. Having seen those people, most of them severely injured, I lost trust in my reality and in knowing where I was.

To test my reality, I wanted to talk to someone. On Oxford Street, I found a crowd of people who were standing there, confused and not knowing what was happening. Why were all the streets closed to the public? I tried to tell someone what was happening, but no one responded. They weren't really interested in conversing. Perhaps they were somewhat used to such disruptions. In those days, Irish terrorists were placing bombs in the most unexpected places.

It took me hours to come back to reality. I even forgot to phone my niece, with whom I was staying at the time. She'd been worried after she heard about the bombing on the radio. She knew I was going to be in that area of the city. We both marveled at my miraculous survival. For me, it was also an experience of something else, some mystery about why I chose that particular table at that particular pub. I have experienced and wondered about this kind of mystery throughout my life.

Another very scary and humbling experience came in Taiwan in September 1999. I'd finished my work the day before, and I was back in my room on the fifteenth floor of a big hotel in Taipei. My luggage was packed to leave the next morning. At 2:45 in the morning, I woke up suddenly. Everything was moving: my bed, the television, and the lamps. Whatever had been on the table was now on the floor.

I'd experienced lots up until then, but never this. I soon realized it was an earthquake. I ran out to the hallway and saw people running toward the stairs. Most of the other hotel guests spoke only Japanese or Taiwanese, so I couldn't talk to them.

Soon Marie, my translator, whose room was nearby, came and told me we'd have to run downstairs. I got dressed quickly, and we ran to the stairs. I was shaking and very much afraid. The fear was different from anything I'd ever felt. The worst was my terror of being buried alive, which happened to many people in that quake.

The stairs were narrow. As we ran down them, everything around us was crumbling and moving. I had no idea what was going to happen next. When we finally got down to the main floor, the lobby was full of children, old people, and other hotel

My son, Andrew Gomori 1992

guests. Nobody knew anything. We had no information, and we didn't know what to do.

There were what seemed like thousands of aftershocks. Whenever the lobby's huge chandeliers started swinging, we all ran out into the street. We were afraid that they'd fall on us. Out on the street, however, I realized I was not going to be safer there. As I saw buildings bending and concrete falling, I became aware that no place was safe.

The lobby had one phone from which I could dial overseas directly. I phoned my son in Canada to tell him that I was okay so far. It was midday for him, and he was in his office with a patient. He hadn't yet heard about the earthquake and, as he told me later, was confused about why I was calling him to say I was fine. I told him what had happened, but it never really sunk in for him until he got home and heard the news.

I'm glad I called him when I did, because later there was absolutely no phone service, even within Taipei. The tremors continued for hours, until the morning. We waited. I didn't know whether I could get to the airport. Before going home, I'd planned to spend three days in Bali. I'd been planning this trip for quite a while. I'd always wanted to see Bali but never before had the time. My darling friend Jerry Lai, the executive director of the foundation I work with, had offered to escort me. I wondered whether he would still pick me up at 6 A.M. Nobody knew what the roads might be like.

Miraculously, Jerry arrived. He came in a taxi and said we could try to get to the airport. I left my luggage in the hotel and arranged for another friend to pick it up later. My plan was to return to Taipei and then fly home to Canada. Fortunately, we got to the airport. Then we found out that the center of the quake was in the middle of the country, not far from Taipei. We checked in and boarded the plane to Bali. As we took off, I was never so happy to be in the air and to leave the earth.

In Bali, Jerry and I were devastated to hear the news of what was happening in Taiwan. Thousands lost their lives; others lost their houses. Of the people who'd been in my workshop, many lived in the area most devastated by the earthquake. For a long time, we didn't know what happened to them.

This was not the vacation I'd looked forward to. I knew I had to go back to Taipei, but the city was still having aftershocks

Marie Lam
1999

daily. I was advised to take another route home, but I decided to follow my original plan, fly back to Taipei, and catch my flight to Canada the next afternoon.

The fear and shock stayed with me the entire time. Jerry and I flew back to Taipei the next day, where I checked into a hotel near the airport and picked up the luggage my friend had kept for me. That night, I was terrified. The hotel was a strange place for me, far from the city and already damaged by the quake. I kept my clothes on, just in case. I studied the stairs and the lobby, and I waited. I've never experienced such a long night.

My friend Marie Lam phoned from Hong Kong to say she'd made it home. After our talk, she alerted other friends in Taipei to call me. Despite their not speaking English, we somehow managed to talk. Again, I experienced these people as very caring and loving, even though they had their own problems.

Being near the airport, the hotel was full of rescue workers from all over the world. These were people who go wherever there's a disaster. Friends who took me to the airport talked to them and found out more of the horrible details.

The quake was a unique experience for me. When the earth shook, I had felt the energy of nature—and I felt very, very small and helpless in this universe. It was the same feeling as when I stood at the Wailing Wall in Jerusalem, an awareness of how insignificant we are in the context of the past and the future.

However, my body had its own reaction after the earthquake, even after I got home and knew I was safe. I kept trembling for about two weeks. I'd survived many things, but the earth had never moved. It was a horrible experience, not being able to trust even that.

After both these escapes from death, people asked whether I had traumatic aftereffects. "Of course not," I answered, surprised. As the rest of this book shows, I'd been through more than my share of dangerous situations. The overwhelming and helpless sense of fear that gripped me during the earthquake was the same feeling I'd had as early as age four. Stepping over dead or injured people in the London pub had been ghastly, but I had also walked through a similar scene in Hungary during World War II.

My past learnings had helped me cope in the present. Some mystery—my spirit guides—has always kept me alive, and I've created powerful learnings out of the many unfortunate experiences since my beginnings.

The family is the vehicle
from whom we learn to be
who we are.

—Virginia Satir

Children see only parts of
their parents.

—Sharon Loeschen

— 2 —

Knots

My world began on May 25, 1920 in Budapest, Hungary. I was an only child living in what now seems like a bizarre world. From our family dynamics to the politics of the day, things then were very different, much more menacing, than what most people experience in childhood.

I grew up with loving and traditional parents, both of whom came from large families. Their religion was Jewish, but they never practiced. Religion was not an important part of my upbringing. My first language was German. When I was born, the Austro-Hungarian monarchy's influence was still affecting the middle class. A "good upbringing" meant speaking German and having

Me as a toddler
1922

German-speaking nannies. I learned Hungarian when I went to school. It was considered the language of peasants, of the lower class.

My mother was the second youngest of six children in a rich and very enmeshed family. Everybody's business was everybody's business. Her mother died when she was six years old, so her

My mother

older sisters raised her. This had great impact for her, and she never really separated from her brothers and sisters emotionally. They came first, and my father and I came second. She spent her inheritance to support her brothers when they were in trouble. The power of her family seemed enormous in my growing up.

Our ideals and values were very different, and my mother didn't understand me. She also talked all the time. I'd simply say yes and no while she went on talking. After awhile, I wouldn't be there, I would tune out. Her wish for me was to get married, have many children, and live happily ever after. When I was sixteen, she insisted that I go to a so-called ball. Sitting on the sidelines in a nice dotted dress, I waited for boys to ask for a dance. Finding that boring and humiliating, I never wanted to be in that position again.

Distorted perceptions can stay with us into adulthood. My perceptions about my mother persisted for a long time. I learned early in life that her other relatives were more important than I

My father

was. She knew how to love her brothers and sisters, but she really didn't know how to be a loving mother to me. Her sisters especially were important for her, and I was jealous of them.

My relationship with my mother affected my later relationships with women. Now, I know she loved me in her own way. But when I was a child, she did not live up to my expectations and I interpreted that as not loving me. I think that experience of loving was what I was missing. And I think that was why I had a very difficult time making female friends. I didn't trust them because I didn't want to be disappointed. Lifelong objectives— or "knots," as R. D. Laing called them in his wonderful book of poems—are shaped in childhood experiences, and untying some of my knots has been an ongoing process in my life. For a long time, I only had male friends; even now, I have only a few women friends I trust.

Trusting men more had everything to do with my father. He was the eldest of five siblings. After he became a lawyer, his sisters and brothers and their children depended on him financially

*My parents and me
1923*

and emotionally. My parents' arguments were always about money and their relatives, so he gave his siblings money secretly. In our immediate family of three, I was always on my father's side. I know now that I did not help their relationship by being between them.

My father was the closest person in my growing up. He loved me unconditionally, and I felt protected. My earliest memory of knowing that he loved me was at age three. My crib was in my parents' bedroom, and I often woke up at night and cried. My mother got angry when this happened, and from this I learned I was not supposed to upset her. My father tied one end of a long string around his wrist and attached the other end to my crib. He taught me to pull it when I woke up at night, and he would pull it back. This comforted me, and I went back to sleep. This was my first experience of having a secret: that he loved me more than my mother. (When I work with people now, I ask them to find out how their children know that they are loved.)

Both my parents' families came from the northern part of Hungary, which had by then become Slovakia. I learned early that Hungary, my country, was always on the wrong side in wars. The first thing I learned in school in the 1920s was that Hungary had been divided after World War I: the north side was annexed to Czechoslovakia, the southern part was ceded to create Yugoslavia, and the eastern part (Transylvania) was annexed to Romania. With anger, we called our country the "amputated Hungary." We learned we would have to fight the whole world to make Hungary one big country again. We learned to hate the Slovaks, Romanians, and Serbs. Similarly, I am sure they were learning to hate Hungarians.

Most of my mother's family lived in the north, in what had become Slovakia. One of my maternal aunts and her husband had a huge pig farm, where I had to spend all my summers. These were painful times in my younger years. All my friends went to the lake for the summer with their parents, but I had to stay with my dreaded cousins Jan, Stephen, and Ladislow.

My fear of them began when I was about four years old, and they were five to eight. Elisabeth Kübler Ross said that during a few events in life, in a critical moment, we set our goals, objectives, and values into a certain direction. I think that is true. One of my moments came while my cousins and I played Indian war games in wild costumes and with toy guns. In the garden, they held me prisoner in a spot surrounded by bushes. When I wanted to go to the bathroom, they gave me a bottle—and then teased me about not even being able to pee into it as they did. This was my first education about gender.

After guarding against my escape during the day, they threatened to hang me if I told the grownups. Terrified, I thought I would be killed at any moment. I was too scared to tell anybody—ever. I felt helpless, frightened, and utterly alone. Each morning, I never knew whether I would survive the day. My passion for freedom, which guided me throughout the rest of my life, started here.

Sometimes, I pretended to be sick, but it never fooled my cousins into relenting. I couldn't simply say no to them, and I didn't stand up to them when I knew I would lose. My only relief came when my father arrived to visit for one or two days. I knew he would protect me. I'd ask him to hold my hand, all day, and my bullying cousins couldn't get near me. In my growing up, my father's love was my only source of knowing that I was okay.

My tormentors played other nasty games. Once, they tied me to a tree. Another time, at night in my room, they put a candle inside a pig's skull, which made a horrible flickering image and frightened me terribly. My constant dread grew even more.

One day, my cousin Jan offered to play a game of chess with me. I felt very privileged. However, the deal was that if I lost, he could cut my long, curly red hair. Of course, I lost. He cut my hair really badly. When the adults saw me, they punished me for being stupid enough to let that happen. How unjust grownups can be, punishing the innocent, the victim.

As we grew older, the struggle with my cousins turned to the area of reading. My cousins were extremely intelligent boys who soon read all the classics in many languages. So for five summers after I turned ten, they gave me a list of books they had already read. I would spend the rest of the year catching up, but by the following summer, they were ahead again. I felt stupid—and I had a daunting new list of books.

Those three boys did everything kids can do to a little girl to invalidate her and lower her self-esteem. Never validated for knowing enough, I really believed that I was not good enough for them. I did not realize how abused I was. My only validation came from my father. I knew he loved me, no matter what.

Even though all this was painful, however, it did help me become extremely curious, competitive, and ambitious about reading and learning. It began out of survival motivations, but by the time I was seventeen, I loved reading. I also wanted to earn their respect by knowing more than my cousins did. So cu-

*My soulmate Steven
1937*

riosity and survival were the two pieces that influenced my search for intellectual growth.

When my cousins started to go out with girls, they didn't take me with them, which increased my insecurity as a woman. The first time I experienced their respect was in 1937 when they invited Steven, their architect friend from England, to spend the summer. (Two of my cousins were then studying at Cambridge.) Steven was the first young man who respected me and talked with me, and we fell in love. This changed my cousins' perceptions of me, and my relationship with them changed into friendship. Steven was the bridge in that.

Before and after he returned to London, Steven and I developed a loving and platonic relationship. I had always wanted to be loved for my soul rather than my body, and Steven agreed with this. Both idealistic, we discussed how we would get married and make the world a better place.

For better or worse, my relationship with Steven and my cousins' new regard for me both unfolded during my last summer at my aunt's farm. That fall, my last year of high school began in Budapest. I was already sure that I did not want to live in Hungary. I did not have a sense of belonging to any culture, religion, or group other than the family. From my earliest memories, I had always wanted to be free. I wanted to be free from my extended family. I wanted to live in a country with political freedom, and I yearned to get away from an environment that was suppressive and unjust. The Hungarian government then was very rightist and dictatorial. Hungary had always been allied with Germany, and by that time, Hitler and Nazism were facts in Europe.

While my cousins studied in Cambridge, I told myself, I would be in Paris. I looked for the most pragmatic way to work toward a job in the United States. In Paris, the Curie Institute offered a four-year course in physics and guaranteed each graduate a job in the United States. I was not interested in physics, but I was obsessed about getting to California, so I decided to do this. Since a Hungarian high school education was considered inferior to that in France, I would first have to take a year at the Sorbonne in chemistry and mathematics. Then I could take an admission exam at the Curie Institute.

When my father found out that I wanted to go to Paris, he was horrified. His concerns were realistic: war was brewing, and I was very naïve. So he set up some roadblocks. I would have to earn straight A's in my last year of school. I would have to speak perfect French. I would have to convert to Catholicism, just to be safe. I would have to earn admission to the Sorbonne. And I had to promise to come back the way I left, as a virgin.

The last condition did not pose a problem for me. During my teen years, I was not interested in boys. The only place I ever met any was at the skating rink. My high school was an extremely traditional and conservative public school for girls. We wore uniforms and—to our dismay—bright red aprons. Next door at the boys' school, they laughed at this outfit.

Being sheltered and naïve, I did not know much about sex. In our home, the subject was never mentioned. My only education about it came from books and pictures that I read secretly with my girlfriends. We decided when we were all seventeen that we never wanted to marry, and that sex would not be part of our lives.

Regarding my father's other roadblocks, my intellectual growth again became a survival tool. Serious study enabled me to meet all the criteria, and he had to let me go. I could now leave Hungary as well as the constrictions of my family. This fulfilled my dreams both as a child and a young adult: to live in freedom.

Looking back at the values and beliefs learned in childhood, I see many things differently now. From my father, I learned honesty, the value of justice, unconditional love, hard work, and an appreciation of life's simple things. For example, my father had his routine: he worked at home, and every afternoon he took a break. He'd go to the nearby coffeehouse to read the papers and to meet friends. He never traveled, saying, "People and houses are the same everywhere." He had no special needs, and his interest was the family. I learned from him to give lovingly and to be consistent with my principles. For a long time, I idealized him. I still tend to idealize the people I feel close to and love.

Up to the age of eighteen, I did not validate myself much at all. That my father loved me meant that perhaps I was a little bit lovable. I also had a few friends. Other than that, I felt insignificant, not very bright, and incapable of doing many things. In every single way, I put myself down. I was a very good student because my parents expected that, but that didn't raise my self-esteem. By and large, I really believed that I was stupid. So I truly know what it means to feel insecure, to have low self-esteem, and to feel totally wiped out by others. This has helped me tremendously in my understanding of other people and in being humble.

With my grown-up eyes, I see my mother in a new way. She had a strong bonding with her siblings, who raised her and represented her parents. I feel sad that she grew up as the Cinderella in her family, and she continued playing that role as an adult. I learned never to do that. When I was young, I saw her extended family as a burden. Their control of her angered me, and they wanted me to live up to their expectations. This influenced me to do the opposite, to develop my own mind and expectations, and to rebel.

Me
Summer 1937

My mother hadn't experienced her own mother, and she could not live up to my expectations for mothering. I used to blame her for that. Now I know that she did the best she knew. I learned from her loyalty to family and her generous way of loving.

I feel sad that I did not know my grandparents and that I grew up as an only child. Maybe the lack of these connections is what fascinates me about families. Meanwhile, as an only child, I learned to be responsible—normally the role of the oldest child. I also learned to feel entitled—the role of both the only child and the youngest one. I did not experience the sharing that siblings learn.

In my experience with my cousins, I learned to survive in the face of fear, to maintain my courage to be, and to struggle with a poor self-image. At the same time, I developed the motivation and determination to prove myself, to learn more, and to be curious. I still maintain that sense of not knowing enough and never catching up. However, this became a driving force for learning, which I value.

From my soulmate Steven, I learned to share. Resonating with his idealism, I learned to accept my own dreams of working toward a better world. That faith and idealism is still with me.

Things don't change, you change your way of looking, that's all.

—Carlos Castañeda

The important thing is not to stop questioning. Curiosity has its own reason for existing. One cannot help but be in awe, when he contemplates the mysteries of eternity, of life, of the marvelous structure of reality. It is enough if one tries merely to comprehend a little of this mystery every day. Never lose a holy curiosity.

—Albert Einstein

— *3* —

Paris 1939

My life in Paris in 1938 and 1939 was an enriching and important experience. I loved the freedom of speech that I experienced for the first time. Every evening, people such as Jean Paul Sartre and Albert Camus talked at the university and in the Luxembourg Gardens. Everything existential was exciting for me, even the dark side. I'm fascinated by Franz Kafka, too. He has a positive darkness, a creative one.

I learned about existentialism in the context of life-and-death struggles in Europe, when the world was burning and we knew that the war was coming. I was happy that the war was coming. It may sound crazy now, but that is the way it was. I knew that the enemy, the Nazis, would have to go, even if we died. Dying for a purpose is not an issue, for me. It's a way of living.

For me, Paris held danger, hope, fear, and absolute intellectual brilliance—all at the same time. These writers didn't talk much about hope, but just knowing that people like them existed, and that we existed along with them, gave me hope that living is worthwhile. It also gave me the idea of fighting, and it helped me go through life doing the unusual.

The intellectual and emotional climate in Paris was dignified, idealistic, and humane. For example, take one tradition regarding political refugees. At that time, more and more people from European countries had fled to Paris without identification papers. Officially, the French police had to check people's documents. However, at least on the Boulevard St. Michel in the city's student quarter, the Quartier Latin, the unwritten rule was that anybody with papers walked along one side while those without used the other side. The police checked only the first side. To me, that and similar experiences demonstrated the humanity of France and the French people.

It was also one of the greatest learnings for me to grow up, to be on my own, and to learn that people are good and bad. At first, I knew many Americans and many Hungarians, but I didn't know many French people. One day, I met a man who started talking with me. He said he had a wife and two children and he invited me for dinner. I thought, "Oh, good, I'm invited to meet a French family." We went to his house, and he led me to the basement. Two huge dogs were there, and he put on music. I didn't see his wife or any children. "Well," I asked, "when are we going to have dinner, and where is the family?"

"Oh, they are upstairs," he replied. "We live separately."

I got scared. How the hell was I going to get out? I was trapped in this basement with these two dogs. I did manage to leave, but I never accepted another invitation from a man unless I saw his wife around. This incident was a terrible disappointment for me about people. I was also disappointed at how stupid and naïve I had been.

To pass my exams, I had to work hard. At first, I lived near the Sorbonne in a little hotel, like many students. Soon, however, I got really sick of my room's dirty walls and so looked for other accommodations. I found a multicultural and multiracial organization called La Cité Universitaire, which had separate buildings for students of many countries, with a common area for food and recreation. Hungary didn't have its own building, of course; luckily, I found a room in the American building, where a woman named Elsa Allan rented me a room and became my first American friend. She was an artist from Los Angeles. Her sister was studying pharmaceutical science, and their mother was living in Paris during their studies.

Elsa was a new experience for me and provided the fun and sophistication in my Paris days—as well as some of my first education about men. Believing that "One can never find everything one wants in one man," she had an English, an American, and a French boyfriend. Her French friend was for sex, the Englishman was for intellectual stimulation, and the American paid the bills. I was afraid of what might happen if they ever met at our apartment, but she was not worried. Apparently, they all knew about each other.

This was very different from my concept of loving and having a boyfriend. From time to time, Steven and I met: he would take a boat to Dieppe, where we spent very romantic weekends full of soul talk and wonderful plans for the future. To sound grownup and to fit in, I lied to Elsa, who wouldn't understand my having a platonic relationship. I also started to smoke. One day, she gave me a box of Jellys for the weekend. When I came back, I told her I ate them. She was horrified. That's when I found out that they were birth control devices.

Meanwhile, I completed my year at the Sorbonne and worked most of the summer in a Swiss kindergarten, where I also studied for my admission exams. I took the test and, in the middle of August 1939, I was admitted to Fall classes at the Curie Institute. Very happy, I saw my whole life going in the right direction. I even had friends from California for when I got to the United States.

*Dieppe
1939*

A couple of weeks later, I hitchhiked to a beach near Dieppe for a weekend with some of my Hungarian friends. On the afternoon of September 1, 1939, the beach suddenly emptied. We soon learned that Germany had invaded Poland. The war had broken out. My first reaction was to celebrate. Finally, someone would stop Hitler. The British no longer needed to negotiate— they would fight. We thought the war would end in three weeks and Hitler would disappear.

Hitchhiking back to Paris that day was difficult. Anxiety and stress filled the air, and drivers didn't want to take us. We finally found a trucker who was delivering carpets, and he got us back to Paris that night. The whole city was dark. The war became real.

Letters had come from my mother, asking me to return home. My parents were concerned about my staying in France during the war. I had no intention of going home instead of starting my studies at the Curie Institute. Elsa and her family decided to leave on the *Queen Mary*'s last crossing to the United States. They wanted to take me with them. Mrs. Allan said I'd be like her third daughter. Here was my great opportunity to get to the States without being a physicist. But I had a change of heart. I was determined to stay and fight and not leave Europe until this war was won.

Meanwhile, all the students were evacuated from Paris. The Curie Institute was resettled in Toulouse. For some reason, however, I was directed to Poitiers, another university town in the west of France. There, for the first time in France, I experienced discrimination and prejudice. In the eyes of people in that small provincial town at the outbreak of the war, anybody who wasn't French became an enemy, especially a Hungarian with long red hair. Hungary was on Germany's side. No landlady would rent me a room. It became real to me that I was an alien in that country, even though I was determined to stay and fight.

I learned to survive in chaos and controversy. Witnessing the invasion and collapse of various countries, I involved myself fully with an existential perspective and believed that we would defeat the enemy. Idealism mixed with total desperation as I embraced a real experience of being.

It was impossible to get to Toulouse, as that meant getting a train back to Paris. All available trains were taking the army east to defend the famous Maginot Line between France and Germany. The belief was that those defenses would serve as a stronghold for France. It soon became clear, unfortunately, that neither the Maginot Line nor the French forces could save us from the German army.

I ran into a South African woman I knew from the Sorbonne who let me stay with her for a few weeks. The landlady of that rooming house was sure that I was a spy, however, and I felt quite uncomfortable. I went to the mayor and told him that I wanted to stay and fight the Germans. He gave me a student card and a gas mask, which I hoped to use when the Germans bombed

France. I was very proud and enthusiastic about contributing to the war in case of an air attack. (After the war, I found out that the Germans never bombed Poitiers.)

Having little money, I lived on sardines and loaves of French bread. As the war went on, I became heavier and heavier and more and more frustrated in Poitiers. Finally, I decided I simply had to get to Toulouse. On my way there, I managed to go through Paris. The city looked dark and sad, and the Germans were threatening to invade it any day.

All the while, my father was sending more and more telegrams demanding that I return to Budapest. Finally, when my mother wrote that he had gone to bed and was not getting up until I returned, I decided to take the Orient Express home for a visit. As a student, I was able to get a visa for returning to France within thirteen days. My father arranged for all the other visas I needed for traveling through Switzerland and Italy.

It was a warm and wonderful visit. Then, on the day I was to leave, he said he would die if I went. His fears were clear to me, and I perceived this as pure love. Only much later did I realize it was also control. My loyalty and love for him wrestled with my values, dreams, and strong desire to return to freedom and to my studies in Toulouse. Having left all my belongings in Paris, I thought my mother would support me in returning to get them. That did not happen. I didn't know whether I could survive the war in France, but I knew that being in Hungary was equally dangerous. I experienced chaos within myself and around me, and a growing anger toward everything. I thought I had no choice but to remain at home and not return to France.

I felt betrayed and helpless, but I stayed. I never found the belongings I had left in France, and I did hear that many of my

Hungarian friends from Paris ended up in concentration camps. Needless to say, I never became a physicist. Nor did I get to the United States the way I had originally planned. But I never gave up the idea that I would live in a free world. My time in Paris had brought me some of the most enriching learnings in my growing up. I learned to be on my own, to fight for freedom, to live in chaos, and to be passionate with my ideas. Being in Paris also shaped my beliefs, my spirit, my dreams for myself, and my hopes for worldwide freedom, peace, and justice.

There are only two ways to approach life—as a victim or as a gallant fighter—and you must decide if you want to act or react, deal your own cards or play with a stacked deck. And if you don't decide which way to play with life, it always plays with you.

—*Merle Shain*

The greatest joy in life is loving one's children, the next greatest being loved by them.

—*Thomas Szasz*

— 4 —

Love, Fear, and Danger

Returning to Hungary in the middle of the war molded the following sixteen years of my life. Resigned to living out the war in Budapest, I taught French to make money. I wanted to continue my university studies as well, but the only possibility for a woman in Hungary was economics. While that subject didn't interest me at all, I enrolled because I had to do something. The university in Hungary was nothing like it had been in Paris, and I hated it. I also hated being in a country that was allied with the Germans.

I felt very much alone. Many of my old friends had left Hungary at the beginning of the war. Elsa Allan, my friend from Paris, continued trying to get me to America. She found me through the U.S. embassy and provided all the papers for me to emigrate. At that time, however, I did not want to leave my parents.

Still dreaming of going to the United States eventually, I wanted to learn English. I found a teacher, Jules Sherrington, who worked for the British embassy. He was from a world to which I wanted to belong and was older than I by eighteen years, wiser, and politically compatible. Soon, we became very good friends and started going out together.

Ours was a platonic relationship, but my father was still horrified. He hated Jules because he was divorced, was British, and might take me away from Hungary. To me, this was a big asset—

an opportunity for my rebellion. Jules and I became engaged. This upset my father so much that, when I came home after dinner with Jules one night, he opened the door and slapped my face. It was the first time in my life that he'd hit me. Glaring at Jules and me, he said: "I do not want my daughter to be seen in pubs at night."

This made no sense, of course. I was twenty-one years old and had lived on my own in Paris. I felt humiliated, helpless, and furious with my father. Still, I realized how angry and concerned he was.

Very soon after, the British broke diplomatic relations with Hungary and the whole embassy moved to Turkey. I didn't want to go with Jules. Instead, we decided to correspond through diplomatic post and then marry after the war. Waiting for that day, I just floated around, hating everything and everybody.

Then, during the worst part of the war, a message came from the Hungarian secret service, telling me to go in for an interview. My father said I would never be released if I went to that terrible place, so I went with great fear. Someone took me to a room, where I trembled as I sat down.

Showing me copies of all the letters that Jules had sent me, the secret police told me that the letters were all coded, that they were not love letters, and that I, too, was a spy. Scared and intimidated, I wondered whether these might indeed be coded messages. In those days, we couldn't be sure of anything. "If you want to survive, you and your family," a man said, "you'll stop corresponding with this person, because he is a spy." He added that if I didn't stop, I would be stopped somehow.

I quit corresponding with Jules and simply remained loyal to our engagement. The war also ended all contact with my London friend Steven. It blew away the rosy dreams that we both had for building a better world.

My idealism about being engaged kept me from dating but I met Benyi László. I have always loved artistic people, and my friends in Hungary were either writers or painters. László was an idealist, a man in love with colors, a poor artist, a painter—a man who, to my father's mind, would never make any money. Again, this was the last person he would have wanted me to marry.

László was beautiful, charming, and filled with love for life. He saw the good, the beautiful, and the divine in everything and everybody, from a flower to a person. From him, I learned to value beauty and art and to enjoy living again. He became my first lover. Our relationship was very romantic—and secret. We often bicycled together, and afterward, I would carry my bicycle all the way up to his fifth-floor apartment. If I left it downstairs, my father might see it and find us out.

My engagement to Jules and my relationship with László felt congruent for me, free of contradiction. My engagement was a prelude to marriage, whereas László and I had a totally different relationship—a romance. Also, I remembered what Elsa had told me in Paris about a woman needing three men in her life. László opened up my curiosity for art and beauty and for being a woman.

When the third man turned up on February 7, 1942, my life changed forever. Given my engagement to Jules and my relationship with László, I hadn't gone to parties since returning from France. Then, when my friend Eva had a party, my mother pushed me to go. Reluctantly, I went. As lots of people milled around, a lovely man came up and introduced himself as Paul.

"I understand you're engaged," he added.

"Yeah, I am." Though feeling no particular excitement, I was relieved that he already knew.

"Tell me about it."

I told him about my wonderful Jules, who was still in Turkey, and that we would eventually move to Britain. Paul listened very attentively, and then we danced all night. A veterinarian in private practice, he was a very good listener—and that was his strategy for connecting with me. As I learned later, he'd bragged to his companion that evening that he could get any woman he wanted. At the party, she challenged him: "Well, try to get Maria. She's not available, she's engaged."

He made a bet that he would dance with me and keep anyone else from getting a chance. He won. A new agenda emerged later, when he took me home at the end of the evening, at 3 o'clock in the morning. He declared, "I'm going to marry you."

"You're nuts. You're crazy!" I replied. "Are all veterinarians crazy?" I'd never met a vet and certainly had never met anybody who said he was going to marry me after one party.

Paul was serious, I discovered. He phoned at least once a day, wanting to take me out for dinner. I resisted. My father, who ran his law office out of our home, finally said, "Go out with this young man. He keeps calling, and I cannot have him occupying the line all the time." My father liked the sound of Paul: he wasn't British, wasn't divorced, and was only eight years older than I.

Curious about Paul's persistence and determination, I finally went out with him. We were very different. His passion was to create quality of life no matter what, and he directed his energy into positive thinking and actions. An optimist, he did not spend energy on problems. He had a great sense of humor, found beauty in the world, loved music, and adored people and animals. From the first day, I felt genuine interest, acceptance, and love flowing toward me. Paul valued me as a person and as a woman, and he had loved me at first sight.

Maybe this was what a marriage should be based on, I soon began thinking as we went to romantic small pubs and listened to gypsy music. Nothing could have been more romantic, and he was charming. My attraction grew and grew. I had never experienced anything like his unconditional love, except from my father. It felt overwhelming. Paul had stormed into my life as a shining prince, and I began to value myself through his love for me. He was the missing part of my soul. I also felt safe. I knew I could have both my freedom and my autonomy within our relationship. It all seemed very mystical to me.

Yet, I was still engaged to Jules. I knew I should end that relationship somehow, but I couldn't correspond with him. Over and over, Paul voiced sympathetic sentiments about how awful this was: "I'm really very sorry to take you away from your fiancé." Again, that was his strategy. He suggested sending a telegram. Still ambivalent, I said I would think about it. Also, I had yet to tell Paul and László about each other.

Two weeks after our first date, my best friend, Susan, invited us over on a Saturday evening. Opening a bottle of champagne, Paul declared, "We're going to celebrate our engagement now."

"Engagement?" I echoed, startled.

"Yes," Paul turned to me. "It's going to be announced in the paper tomorrow."

I was stunned. I hadn't even met his family. He explained that because the war was on and he might be drafted, we had to marry very quickly. Somehow, it seemed very funny. I had not planned to get married until after the war—let alone to him— but it was a case of following the process. He convinced me that our marriage was already written in heaven. And now it would be written in tomorrow morning's paper.

That fait accompli would be a disaster for my very conservative father. He would not be at all pleased to hear about it first from the Sunday paper. As much as he liked Paul, I knew he would prefer to meet Paul's parents, mull over the engagement for a year, and plan the wedding carefully. Not daring to face him, I stayed at Susan's, where Paul phoned me the next morning to say he'd told his mother. "What did she say?" I asked. He replied that she had cried all night. A fine beginning.

Then, having seen the paper, my father phoned: "What is this?"

I explained I hadn't known about it, that Paul had put the announcement in the paper. My father said, "This is really terrible. We don't even know his family. You'll have to invite them around this afternoon." Although he sounded very angry, I think he also felt relieved, because he asked what I was going to do about "the other guy," meaning Jules. I said I didn't know because I hadn't been able to contact him yet.

That afternoon, we met with Paul, his mother, and his younger sister, Elisabeth. (His father was dead, and Paul's older sister lived in London.) It wasn't very nice. His mother was not at all delighted about his decision to marry. First, Paul was the family breadwinner, with an elegant little animal hospital that catered to people's pets. As Budapest did not have many vets, his clients included prominent people, such as the family of Zsa Zsa Gabor. Making good money, he spoiled his family.

Second, they had expected that he would remain single until after his eighteen-year-old sister married. Daughters had to marry first, according to tradition. On top of all this, I wasn't even rich. So my mother-in-law didn't like me, didn't like our engagement, and didn't like the whole situation.

At that point in my life, I didn't care about such things. Paul had swept me off my feet, and he didn't care, either. We just wanted to get married. Knowing that he would be drafted, Paul insisted on holding the wedding in March. Later, he and I went to the post office and composed a long telegram to Jules. I told him that I had met Paul and that I was very sorry, but with life being so uncertain, Jules and I might well never see each other again. I was going to marry Paul instead.

Everything happened so fast. When László phoned a few days later, I told him that I wouldn't see him because I was getting married. "Just like that? You are running out of my life," he said. (He would repeat this statement a few more times over the next fifty years.)

Paul and I met on February 7 and married on March 29, 1942. We had a civil wedding. My father cried throughout. For our weeklong honeymoon, we went to a beautiful hotel in the mountains. Everything was just wonderful and romantic. The

Our wedding day
March 29, 1942

Me with Paul on our wedding day
March 29, 1942

very last evening, we had some money left from what my father had given us. Paul invited everybody in the hotel to share our happiness and celebrate with champagne. The next day, we arrived home without enough cash for the taxi. I felt great.

Soon after, I saw a gynecologist, a good friend of Paul, to find out how to protect myself from getting pregnant. Those very hard times in the midst of war were not when we wanted to get pregnant. By then, our German "allies" practically ruled Hungary, and Germany was all over Europe. However, the gynecologist told me it was too late. I was already pregnant.

The news turned my whole family absolutely upside down. My parents didn't believe in abortion, but the situation was so bad that none of us knew whether we would live through the war. This child might never have a father. British bombs were falling in Budapest and all over Hungary, and we spent lots of time in cellars.

Even though we faced death, however, we welcomed those bombs. They hit railways running toward Poland and the enemy. By then, the Germans had deported most Jewish people living outside Budapest. Paul was Jewish, and his sister and mother disappeared one day from their house on the outskirts of Budapest. I ran everywhere, from the police to various government offices to the clergy, but nobody gave me any information. I could find out nothing about where they had gone. I went home feeling frightened and desolate.

My mother's sister—the mother of my three cousins—came down from the north for a family meeting about my pregnancy. It was always my mother's family that wanted to decide my life. I just sat there, listening to everybody. Even though they didn't believe in abortion, they decided, I should have one. I didn't agree. I knew it was useless to argue with the family or stand up to them, or even to be open with them. I knew what I had to do. I was in love with Paul, and I wanted to have that baby. Nobody was going to abort this child.

On May 29, 1942—exactly two months after our wedding, and when I was two months pregnant—Paul was drafted along with a group of young professional Jewish men. In Hungary, the Germans forced Jewish men of military age to perform manual work in labor camps where conditions were as harsh as in prison. They were treated worse than animals. During Germany's inva-

My mother and her siblings, 1934
(standing) Solti Margit, Donath Terez (my mother),Horvath Ilka;
(sitting) Tauber Sandor, Gross Szeren, and Tauber Lajos

sion of the Soviet Union in June 1941, they were sent to the front, where they faced even more hardship and death. As the German army advanced, burning and raping on their way, they always filled their front lines with troops from Hungary and their other satellite countries. In front of the army were these groups of Jewish men, whom the German and Hungarian generals regarded as expendable.

We heard that Paul's group would be in the most vulnerable position: picking up mines that the Russians were scattering as they retreated from the Germans. The day before their departure, Paul's transport gathered at a train station on the outskirts of Budapest. Wives and relatives were allowed to come and see them

Me while pregnant
1942

off. The general in charge told us very bluntly to say goodbye forever, because these men would never come back. I will never forget or forgive that day.*

Paul knew about the pregnancy. Before he left, he said, "You will have to decide by yourself. I have to leave, and I am helpless. You decide what you want to do. I would like to have my son." He said he knew it was going to be a boy.

Abortion was not legal in Hungary then, but we knew of one doctor who did abortions. My mother made an appointment for us to see him. Before that day, I called him, saying, "I'm coming in with my mother, but I don't want this abortion, so you must say something to convince her that I cannot have it. If you don't, I will have you charged." My intent was to threaten the hell out of him.

He did very well. After examining me, he showed my mother various books full of pictures of all the horrible things that can happen during an abortion. I might never have another baby, he cautioned. All this persuaded her to change her mind. The family left me alone to have the baby. My parents even gave me support. It was very risky, all the same. Paul was gone, and times were difficult.

During the next seven months, I became absolutely terrified thinking about my delivery. What was going to happen? How was this child going to come out of me? Terrified, I couldn't talk about it with anybody. Sitting on the bus or streetcar, I would look around at people and think, "They were all born. They all had mothers. I'll survive."

---

* After the war, at the Nuhrenberg trials, this man was sentenced to hang for his war crimes. I went to see his execution. I am not proud to say that I was happy. This is what the war did to me at that time. I had enormous sadness, pain, and anger.

When my contractions began on January 9, 1943, my mother went with me to the hospital. It was the height of the bombing. My contractions were five minutes apart when I heard people whispering about what was happening with the war. I could tell that they didn't want me to know, but I persisted. That's when I found out about the turnaround in the battle of Stalingrad. For the first time, the Russians had pushed back successfully. Along much of the eastern front, they had halted German forces and forced them to retreat. This was a disaster for the Nazi war machine—its first major reversal.

I was very happy at this news. At the same time, I was terribly worried about what might be happening to Paul. This withdrawal meant real danger for the Hungarian army and everybody on Germany's front lines. Paul and his group were in a very dangerous position.

In the middle of labor, I passed out. The birth process stopped until I came to. Looking around, I saw a circle of faces. No one was breathing. "What's happening?" I asked. They said I'd had a heart attack. Fortunately, my gynecologist—Paul's friend—happened to be there and gave me an injection right away. This was utterly unexpected, as I'd never had a heart condition. The doctor soon gave me another injection to restart the delivery, and my son Andy was born at 6 o'clock that night, weighing a healthy seven or eight pounds.

His birth was a miracle for me. Looking into his eyes, I connected with his spirit and with Paul. Awe filled me, and I had no pain any more—only worries about Paul. "Will this baby have a father?" Determined to keep Andy alive, I knew I would never be alone again.

I knew what being loved was because of my father, but I had never loved until I learned how from Paul. I married him because

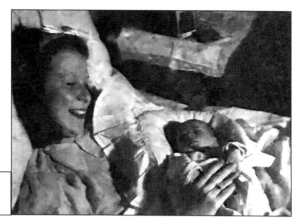

*Andy's birth
January 10, 1943*

his loving was so overwhelming and a whole new experience for me. In addition, I now learned a whole new kind of love from having a baby.

As soon as I could, I had Andy baptized in the Roman Catholic Church so that his papers would say that he was not Jewish. I knew that this might not make any difference to the Nazis, but I did it anyway, just to do whatever I could to keep my son safe. My friend Susan became his godmother.

In Hungary in those days, we breast-fed our babies. Unfortunately, my milk was what we called "nervous," but I didn't know any better. I was twenty-three and had never had a baby before. Andy kept losing weight, so my pediatrician told me to feed him every four hours, then every two hours, then every hour. I did what he said, but I knew something was terribly wrong. The more Andy nursed, the more he threw up. By the time he was three months old, he weighed less than when he was born. While he had grown in length, he was in a terrible state. His eyes were like those of an old man and his body was covered in eczema. They treated that externally, but he continued to lose weight. He looked terrible. No one could tell me what was the matter with my son.

Feeling very scared, helpless, and sad, I took him to the hospital. The first hospital refused to take him overnight, saying they wouldn't take the risk. He was dying. I went to another hospital where another doctor, a wonderful man, admitted him and reversed the pediatrician's treatment. Knowing that Andy's problem was internal and had damaged his stomach, he didn't want me to keep breast-feeding. He told us that if Andy stopped losing weight, we could save his life. It would be a slow process.

He did gain weight slowly, ounce by ounce and day by day. The doctor put him on tranquilizers and kept him warm in an incubator. We bottle-fed him human milk that my father bought on the other side of the city. Over and over, despite the bombing, he made his way to and from the wet nurse.

After three weeks, we couldn't afford to keep Andy in the hospital. We had no income, as neither my father nor I could work anymore, and we had nothing left to sell. When I said I wanted to take Andy home, our wonderful doctor offered to come by every day. We couldn't afford that, either, but I knew Andy would not survive without this man. When I asked him to reduce his fee, he said, "I'm not going to come for less, but you can pay me after the war. I want to save this child. He is not only yours—this child is mine, too. We are going to save him." His words have stayed with me forever. They meant that we would survive to see an end to the war.

Andy was in that incubator for six months in our fourth-floor apartment. My parents often babysat. So did László, who had become a really great friend. Whenever the British were bombing, we had to take Andy out of the incubator and down into the cellar. Sometimes bombs fell two or three times a night. The basement was not equipped as a bunker, so we never knew whether we'd make it back up. My greatest fear was that we'd be buried alive after a bomb hit the building. To me, that was a nightmarish thought.

In spite of the danger, we were happy to think that the bombs might be hitting German troops and the rail lines going to Auschwitz. We had heard stories about a labor camp at Auschwitz by 1943, although we did not know the Germans were killing people with gas.

Andy, age 1, and me
1944

On March 19, 1944, eleven German tank divisions rolled into Hungary. Our status changed from "allied country" to "occupied Nazi Hungary." This sealed the fate of Hungary's Jewish community. The arrival of German forces boosted local Fascist groups, and anti-Semitic activity soared throughout Budapest. The Hungarian Nazi party, called the Arrow Cross, came to power under the auspices of the Gestapo, **the** German secret state police. They arrived with a list of people to take away: scientists, writers, and others who made up the cream of our people. The authorities ordered banks and other financial institutions to freeze all assets belonging to Jews, who also had to register all property and valuables. As Steven Spielberg documented in his film The Last Days, deporting and killing Jews—the "final solution"—was still a priority for Germany and in Hungary even though Germany was clearly losing the war. Occupying Nazis forced every Jew to wear the yellow star and to live in designated yellow-star houses. This made access easy when it was time for mass deportations.

The Germans had already transported Jewish people from all over Hungary to Auschwitz. Adolf Eichmann had determined that roundups and deportations should begin in the east and work westward, ending with the capital. He reasoned that the eastern zones were most threatened by the Red army and were home to most of the country's Jewish population. Removing the Budapest Jews was another matter. In certain areas of the city, some people had been taken away earlier, including Paul's mother and sister. This intensified after the German occupation in 1944. The "final solution" focused on Budapest, and we learned firsthand about the horrors of Nazism. I learned about fear and danger, and I learned to survive.

A yellow star hung on the house in which Andy and I were living. Although we could have moved, as I had converted to Catholicism before I went to France, we didn't. If news about

Paul ever arrived, that's where I would get it. In addition, the friends who lived in our house couldn't go out after six o'clock, and I'd run errands for them during their curfew.

That autumn, the Nazis began removing Jews from Budapest. On October 20, 1944, they ordered all Jews aged sixteen to sixty to report for labor service. At 5:30 one November morning, men from the Arrow Cross and German Nazis came to every house in our neighborhood and told us to come out. "Everybody is going." This was not exactly a surprise. Each day, they took groups of men and women from the yellow-star houses. Ultimately, 35,000 of us were moved to camps and to the brick factories on the outskirts of Budapest.

When I protested that I had a baby sleeping upstairs, a Nazi said, "Bring the baby or leave it." Andy was almost two years old, and this decision tore me apart. I couldn't go back for him. "When he wakes up," I thought, "he knows enough about his environ-ment to realize that nobody is there." My parents lived nearby, and I desperately hoped and prayed they would find him before the Nazi caretaker found him.

With guns pointed right at us, I marched through Budapest with others from the surrounding yellow-star houses. There was no way to resist. If anyone tried, the Nazis shot without worrying about doing that right in front of our eyes.

All I could think about was what was going to happen to Andy. Meanwhile, they marched us out of the city to a big brick factory where they had already gathered thousands of others. Because the Allies were bombing railways that ran toward the East, the Germans could no longer transport us by train. Instead, they sent daily groups of thousands onto the 200-mile highway to Austria and, beyond that, toward Germany. Thousands of the Jews on these death marches—more than 70,000 in all—perished in miserable conditions on roadsides, in barns, or in makeshift camps along the way. Others were shot. Those who survived ended up in Mauthausen, Buchenwald, and other concentration camps.

On November 8, the army ordered about 2,500 of us to march toward Austria. They told us that we were going to Germany, to one of the concentration camps. There was no way out. Soldiers, policemen, and German and Hungarian Nazis were everywhere, guarding and leading us on horseback and bicycles. Old or young, we had to walk. Later, some people have asked, "Why didn't people resist?" But anyone who stopped or tried to escape was shot on the spot. The guards also shot babies and mothers on the way. If I had taken Andy, we would have been killed. I never saw such cruelty and humiliation. I wouldn't have believed it possible.

People also died of starvation or exposure along the road. It was cold and snowing already, and we had no food or warm clothes. On either side of us were Germans and Hungarians keeping close watch. We even had to urinate in front of them.

At each of the few towns between Budapest and the Austrian border, we stayed the night in large, fenced enclosures for animals. Every morning, our captors told us there was no way back and promised to kill us if we tried to escape. We couldn't return along the same road because everyone would know that we'd escaped from a transport.

Each day's march started at daybreak so as to arrive at the next town before dark, which in November fell quite early . My friend Eva was in the same transport, and we soon met up. "Eva," I kept whispering to her, "we have to escape." I thought about this all the time. With each passing day, we were farther from Budapest. Getting home was going to be increasingly difficult.

I had to get back to Andy, and I knew I would die if I con-tinued on the march. Eva thought it was too risky. Of course, she didn't have a baby and wasn't married then. Her notion was to survive by going along with what was happening. All the same, we stuck together, holding hands. Toward the end of the third day's march, I said, "Let's stay at the rear and see what happens."

It was pitch black by the time we arrived at the enclosure for that night. I watched closely. Ahead, the guards with their guns were pushing everybody into the pen. It was dark and almost totally silent. Across the way was a barn. In that moment, I made the most important choice of my life. I do not know how or why, but I knew I'd rather die than go on. My only chance was to sneak into that barn. Holding Eva's hand tightly, I dropped down. Then we crawled into the dark. We managed to reach the barn without anyone noticing. All around us was silent. I had no idea what to do next.

I did not know how to get back to Budapest. We couldn't go back by road. Nor could we seek shelter in a village, because everybody was against us. After centuries of deep splits among themselves, we Hungarians didn't necessarily help—let alone trust—each other. "What do we do now?" asked Eva. "Now we are dead. What are we going to do?"

Suddenly, we heard footsteps. It could have been a German soldier. It could have been a Hungarian Nazi. Not knowing, I crawled toward him in spite of my terror. "Can you help us?" I whispered desperately.

"Wait here until I come back," the man answered. For a few minutes, we thought we'd be killed. He would give us up to the army, and we'd be shot. We had seen that often over the past three days.

The man returned, accompanied by another guy. One of them grabbed me, the other grabbed Eva, and we all ran toward the fields. These two guys turned out to be Jews from a nearby labor camp. Knowing that their wives were in our transport, they had hoped somehow to see them and maybe save them. Just when they'd given up because it was so dark, I had approached them, so they saved us instead.

They took us to their camp and had us crawl through a window. No one there needed to ask where we had come from. As Eva and I washed ourselves, I found that my feet were bloodied from walking.

The men said we had to get away from there. They gave us directions on how to go through the fields to the nearest train station, at Dorog. We found it, but it was a small station, and we discovered that the only trains that day were going west, toward Germany. The Soviet army was approaching Budapest, and only soldiers on military trains could go east, toward that city. So we were stranded.

As we sat on the platform, some officers showed up and began asking people for identification. We had no papers. My heart sank. We'd come this far and maybe for nothing. At that moment, spying a group of soldiers, I turned to Eva: "Let's go negotiate with them." We put on our most seductive ways—she with her very good looks, and I with my long red hair—and went over to them.

"Could you spare any cigarettes?" I asked, striking up a conversation. Then I improvised a touching story about how we'd come here looking for somewhere to live because we hated and feared the Russians. We loved the Hungarians and the Germans, but we also had babies at home. "We have to get back now," I told them, "but we're stuck because there are no trains. We have no money, but could you sneak us onto this military train?" I hinted that we would show them a good time when we got to Budapest. Under those circumstances, we were ready for anything. More interested in our flirting than our story, they got us on the train. Hidden under a bench seat, we were on our way home. When we arrived, we got off the train and just disappeared into the depot's confusion.

I couldn't believe that we had actually returned from the death march. Looking back, I now put it down to my spirit guides and guardian angels. Even back then, I did not take credit for it. I just knew that this had not happened solely because of me. Something had guided me, both when I approached the man outside the barn and when I spotted the soldiers at the station. Even the story I made up felt inspired rather than thought out. From then on, I had even more faith in my life's process.

Eva and I couldn't go back to our yellow-star houses. With nowhere to go, we were afraid that everyone could tell who we were from the way we looked and the way we sounded. It was written all over us that we were coming from a death march. Not wanting to endanger my parents, I went to the house of my godparents, who weren't Jewish. I sent Eva to a woman who had worked for Paul and who adored us. She would do anything for us, I knew, even though her husband was a Nazi. Indeed, she was very good, and she hid Eva.*

My godparents, on the other hand, were quite a disappointment. When I got to their apartment building, the concierge exclaimed, "Oh, Jesus Christ, where did you come from?"

---

* Only recently, Eva told me that she was in hiding there for three days. Then László found her a place to stay.

"Just let me in," I said, rushing in. When my godfather opened his door and saw me, I could see the fear and hesitation on his face. As a very good friend of my family, he pulled me inside. As a policeman, he was terrified about my being there. "I tried very hard to get you out," he told me. "I heard from your father, but I couldn't do anything."

"I know. But what you can do now for me is to let me stay here for one night. I'll leave tomorrow, but I have no place else to go." If I spent the night wandering the streets, the police would pick me up immediately.

My godfather reassured me that Andy was with my parents. That was the most important thing. My father had heard about the roundup soon after I left. In Budapest, everybody phoned everybody else right away whenever anything happened. As soon as he heard, my father had run over and picked up Andy.

Despite the risk, my godparents let me stay the night. I left the next day and never saw or spoke with them again. I just couldn't accept how afraid they were to give me shelter for one night. Circumstances injected the same fear into everybody. People who helped a Jew or anybody who was against the system was deemed culpable, too. I understand that fear, but I still cannot accept their behavior. I would not call that being Christian, which is what they claimed to be. This experience reinforced the idea that I could not believe or depend on anyone but myself. I learned to follow my intuition, to believe in my strength, and to carry all the responsibility for Andy and for me.

Back out on the streets, I still did not want to risk going to my parents' house. They had gotten shelter in one of the designated Swedish houses, the Raoul Wallenberg project that saved thousands of Hungarian Jews at the time.

Luckily, I learned from my friend Susan that the Red Cross ran a shelter in a big villa across the Danube in Buda, the part of the city that spreads toward the mountains to the west.

I went to see Paul's employee—the woman hiding Eva—and she agreed to bring Andy from my parents' house. I waited anxiously. Then joy and gratitude flooded me as I saw her wheeling Andy's stroller down the street. I felt immense relief as I gazed at him for the first time in many days.

Without faith, nothing is possible. With it, nothing is impossible.
        —Mary Mcleod Bethune

Only those who risk going too far can possibly find out how far one can go.
        —T. S. Eliot

— 5 —

Surviving Chaos and Confusion

Budapest is a beautiful city divided by the River Danube. In those days, many lovely bridges connected the city's two parts. Pest lies on the river's eastern side, toward Russia, and has the city's financial and commercial sections. From the western bank, Buda spreads over small mountains toward Austria and the rest of Europe. It is the older part of Budapest and features the royal castle (now a museum) and vast residential areas.

Andy and I moved into the Red Cross shelter, located in the basement of a villa in Buda. Full of women and children, it offered sanctuary but not much shelter. Hungarian and Russian soldiers—and later, German ones—sometimes came in and took our food. Or they would just shoot through the windows into the rooms. By the end of the war, Andy's crib was full of holes.

Nobody there knew anyone else's real identity, as we all had false papers. The woman hiding Eva had given me the papers of her daughter, Mezes Panni, who had committed suicide as a teenager. According to these papers, I was eighteen and unmarried. Keeping Andy's real papers and the regulation nametag around his neck, I would pass him off as my nephew. That way, Paul would be able find him even if I was killed. The false papers meant, sadly, that I had to teach Andy not to call me Mama. It broke my heart to tell my two-year-old son, 'I am not your mama. I am Aunty Panni." It was crucial for him to learn this. Every so often, German or Hungarian Nazis would show up at the shelter demanding, "Who are these people?"

"You have no right to ask us who we are," I'd snap back like a tigress. "We are all sheltered by the Red Cross." Taken aback, they would leave. I really enjoyed that role. Filled with defiant energy, I became as arrogant and aggressive as you can imagine. Having escaped and returned from the death march, I wasn't afraid of anybody. I had a strong sense that something out there, beyond, wanted me to live. I had convinced myself that no one could touch me. Fortunately, that turned out to be a good way to deal with the Nazis. Whenever I showed a high level of self-esteem, they responded with a grudging respect. My anger and my ability to rebel against everything helped me feel more secure about myself. They also helped me fight to survive.

The very fact that I survived led me to a kind of spiritual sense of my being, in spite of being an atheist at that time. I had energy within me, which came from somewhere else, from a spiritual place. It gave me a sense of security that wasn't based on knowing a lot. It also helped me get over my low self-esteem. Nowadays, I put it down to my spirit guides, my guardian angels.

Buda and Pest
1992

Even now, that's where I get all my energy. As Pierre Teilhard de Chardin said: "We are not human beings having a spiritual experience . . . we are spiritual beings having a human experience."

Hungary was the last German stronghold in Europe toward the end of 1944, and Soviet troops already occupied the country's western part. To escape the advancing Red army, the Germans and Hungarian Nazis retreated to Buda. Still convinced that Hitler would win the war, they thought the move was only temporary. Then, on January 17, 1945, solders of the Red army liberated Pest, the city's eastern part. Across the Danube at the shelter, we had less and less food every day. Our situation grew desperate. Andy was hungry, and all he said was, "Bread." Shots came through the window constantly. I was afraid. With Andy in my arms all the time, we developed a symbiotic relationship.

The fear was that the war would end but our side of the river would still be a small and forgotten stronghold of the German army. What a nightmare. The German soldiers stationed in that area believed that reinforcements would arrive to help them win. Meanwhile, they brought their wives and children to stay at our shelter. They had food, but these women did not give anything to our starving children. One night, I stole a jar of honey from one of them and fed Andy the whole thing. God punished me: Andy got very sick from eating it on an empty stomach.

Finally, in the middle of February1944, the German officers blew up their bunker and surrendered to the Soviets. The war in Hungary ended, and the USSR occupied our country. In the shelter, we found this out one evening when Soviet soldiers appeared at the door. From their body language and their looks, we instantly knew they had come to rape us. Spontaneously, we Hungarian women pointed toward the German military wives standing in one corner and said in one voice, "Take them." They did. (We found out later that these first occupying troops had permission to rape, steal, or kill whatever they chose because Germans had done the same as they invaded the Soviet Union.)

Terrified of being raped, I decided to leave the next morning. I thought it would finally be safe for me to return to my parents' house. After almost two months in the shelter, Andy was hungry and terribly sick. So everything felt urgent. I had no idea what I was getting into, however, as I put Andy in his stroller and walked out of the villa.

I will never forget what I saw in the streets: a dead horse here, an eye there, and an arm nearby. It was a battlefield. Notices on the walls apparently announced that Buda was still a war zone and no civilians were allowed on the streets for the next forty-eight hours. These were written in Russian, however, so I did not know this at the time.

I headed for the nearest bridge. It would be the shortest route to my parents' place in Pest. But it was gone. I went to the next bridge, and then the next. They were all gone. Slowly, it dawned on me that the retreating Nazis had blown them up, hoping to delay the Russians from occupying Buda.

The Danube looked frozen, but I was afraid to go across with the stroller. Cold and hungry, I walked all day until I reached the city's outskirts. It had been stupid to leave that shelter, and stupid not to go back once I saw what had happened on the streets, but I felt I had to go forward. Around 5 o'clock that dark February evening, I saw a temporary military bridge. As I approached, a young soldier asked, "What are you doing here?"

A Hungarian-speaking person in a Russian tank—immediately, I trusted him. "I have to get across to the other side." I explained that Andy needed food and medicine, and that I was trying to get to my parents' house.

"Civilians are not allowed on this bridge. But if you give me your watch, I'll take you across." Later, I heard that Russian soldiers collected watches because they didn't know about winding them. When a watch stopped, the story went, they just got a new one. He added, "The kid mustn't cry."

"If you give me a piece of bread," I told him, "then he won't cry." It was the first food Andy had eaten in days.

The soldier got us into his tank and covered us with all sorts of stuff so that he wouldn't get caught. Once we got across the bridge, he turned left instead of right as I had requested. Heading away from the city, he drove awhile and finally stopped somewhere in the northern part of Pest. I didn't know where we were. He lifted the stroller out, got me out, and started running toward a small farmhouse. I ran after him into the house. The soldier just left me there in the kitchen, where a woman muttered, "Jesus Christ, they're coming back." She turned to leave.

"Please don't go," I begged. "Stay with me." I needed to find out where I was and how soon I could begin the last part of my journey home.

"No," she said, "they bring women here every night." I realized that after running away from being raped in Buda, I had landed in the same possibility in Pest.

Soon another soldier entered. He looked German with his blond hair, and he spoke fluent German, but he was a Soviet officer. He began interrogating me in a room next to the kitchen. I was fluent in German, which made him suspect I was a spy. "Give me the names of all the people hiding in the area," he demanded. He was referring to those from the Nazi government. I said I would love to, but I had no idea. He asked for my papers, and I told him my story. Unfortunately, I could prove nothing.

Andy's papers identified him as Andy Gomori. My papers showed a different last name. Everything about me seemed suspicious.

"Take me to my parents. They will prove everything."

But he wasn't taking me anywhere. I couldn't convince him that I didn't know anything. His suspicion was well reasoned, of course. Here I was, breaking curfew on the first day after Buda's "liberation," with a child who was not mine. There had to be something terribly wrong with me. The more we talked, the more obvious it was that I had absolutely no way of explaining myself. I couldn't believe that I had gotten myself into such a situation— and just as the war was ending. Ever since that night, I've hated the Russians. I was disappointed, and I didn't believe in them. I felt that, for me, that World War III had already begun, no matter how the current one turned out. By not believing who I was, my liberator became my enemy.

The officer refused to believe that I was not on the side of the Germans. I told him my husband was in a German concentration camp. He sneered, "Oh yeah, now everybody's been in a concentration camp. And everybody's our friend. Everybody's against the Germans." By this point, he saw whatever I told him as a made-up story. "You're a prisoner, and this is war. I want you to know that." He was about to leave me under the guard of two soldiers who were sitting and eating in the kitchen.

I called out to them: "This child is hungry, can he have something?"

"There's no food," they responded.

The officer left, saying, "I'll give you until 2 o'clock in the morning to make a list of the people. If you don't, we'll take you to headquarters, where you'll be raped in front of your son."

Sitting there in terror for hours that night, I would have killed Andy and myself if I had found some method for doing that. I saw no way out. My disappointment was bitter and over-whelming. It was the first day of liberation, and I was a prisoner of the Russians. I couldn't believe what was happening. I wanted to die.

Around 2 in the morning, somebody knocked softly on the window next to me. It was the soldier who had brought me across the river in his tank. When I opened the window, he said, "You didn't give me the watch."

Turning into the tigress, I blasted at him: "I'd rather swallow that watch than give it to you. You cheated me. You betrayed me. You brought me here. If you have a gun, kill my boy and me. Then you can have my body and my watch. But you'll kill us both first."

I don't know what happened to him, but he said, "I'm really worried for you. The whole army stationed here is going toward Germany, and they're going to take you along as their prisoner."

"So kill me," I demanded, "That's what I want. You did this. You finish it."

"In a few minutes, they're going to come for you. I'll lift the stroller out, and I'll let you go if you give me your watch." He must have felt guilty. So he lifted Andy out the window, and I climbed out in a hurry. When I gave him my watch, he told me to run. I had nothing to lose.

To this day, I don't know how I got home. I was completely out of my body. In that life-threatening situation, my childhood ability to tune out while my mother talked had again served me well. I had started to run and somehow knew, subconsciously, which road to follow along the river and then which other roads and turns to take. I don't remember anything.

Because the Russians were still raping women in Pest, Hungarian men were guarding the locked doors of their apartment houses. That day happened to be my father's turn to stand guard. By then, my parents had moved back home from the Wallenberg house that was protected by the Swedish government. Having spent the most dangerous part of the war under that protection saved the lives of my parents as well as many others. They can thank Raoul Wallenberg for their escape.

Suddenly, at 3 in the afternoon, Andy and I were standing in front of my father. I must have walked for twelve hours, since 2:30 in the morning. That was about when the soldier who came back for my watch had lifted Andy's stroller through the window. My father opened the gate for us, he told me later, but I was in a terrible state and speechless.

Two days later, I woke up to find everybody looking at me. Around my bed were a doctor, my mother, and my father, their faces pale with concern. During my recovery, I had even more faith in something higher than I, although I didn't know what it was. This was the second time I had escaped. Why had the Russian soldier returned for the watch? Why had the two labor-camp men saved Eva and me after we slipped away from the German death march? My strength, courage, faith, anger, naïveté, rebellion, and determination to survive led me out of a German transport and a Russian hostage situation. My survival experience with my baby was a miracle. Again, that led me to an even stronger spiritual sense of my being. I knew the credit for this escape didn't go to me; I had just taken one step after another. Instead, I gave credit to something beyond myself to which I was connected spiritually. I know now I had guides watching over me.

Now that Andy and I had survived this experience, I somehow knew that Paul was alive, too. We had gotten only one letter from him, much earlier, which had been smuggled to us somehow. So we didn't know where he was—only that he was on the front lines of fire. The letter came before Andy was born, but Paul addressed it to him, saying he was the luckiest person to be born, because he was our child and represented our love for each other.*

Andy was very ill. His eczema had returned, he was not eating, and he was fearful. He didn't recognize either of my parents. I phoned the wonderful doctor who had saved his life as an infant. Already pretty well reestablished in his hospital, he admitted Andy and gave him penicillin baths and injections. That was my son's third rescue from death. He was only two.

His emotional rescue came next, when this doctor referred me to a psychiatrist for Andy. Having seen my constant fear about how we were going to survive, he now lived in fear of abandonment. Whenever I walked away, he screamed and clung to me. He wouldn't even stay with my mother for a minute. I was very worried but did not know what to do. So Andy's work with the psychiatrist involved learning that it was safe to be away from me. All that he had experienced was very disturbing for a child. My abandoning him when the Nazis took me on the death march had a huge impact on him, even though it was at an unconscious level. Then, at the shelter, I had taught him that I was his aunt. He was totally confused about this, because he knew I was his mother.

The work was a very interesting process, as I look back. I didn't know anything about a child's need to learn about separating from his mother, to feel safe in exploring, and to learn to trust. So the three of us played together for one or two sessions before the psychiatrist asked me to go to the next room while he

---

* I wish I could have taken that letter with me when I left Hungary, and I'll always regret that Andy doesn't have it now.

kept playing with Andy. Then I would come back, leave again, and come back again. He repeated this process so Andy could learn that I would return. Then the psychiatrist asked me to go shopping. He told Andy, "Mama goes shopping, and she will come back." At first, he screamed and yelled, but soon he trusted me to return. A while later, the psychiatrist suggested that I move away from my parents, back to where Andy and I had lived by ourselves.

The war in Europe ended in May 1945. I decided to stay in Hungary until I could find out whether Paul was alive. Then we would go to England, where Paul's older sister, my three cousins, and my aunt were living.

Within a few weeks, some of the people coming back from concentration camps told me that when Axis forces retreated from the Russian army, the Germans put surviving Jewish soldiers into various concentration camps in Germany. Paul had ended up in Buchenwald. While we had all feared that he might have died on the front lines, it turned out that he had taken care of the horses, which were kept in the rear. Later, his being a vet also let him survive Buchenwald, where one of the **Schutzstaffel** (SS) men needed a vet to treat his dog's broken leg.

Paul treated the dog slowly, deciding that the leg was not going to heal until the war ended. He already knew that the Americans had landed. It may not be a very nice story about a vet, but it was a smart choice for Paul. He knew how to live life; he did not focus on problems. His beliefs helped him survive under all circumstances. He got extra pieces of potato or bread, which he always shared with a few others. One of his other privileges was that he didn't have to go out to work. Instead, he was supposed to clean the officers' washroom. Each day, however, he secretly put a little white cement into the toilet bowl instead of cleaning it. He was praying that the Americans would get there before it got full.

With the Americans advancing ever closer, the Germans took Buchenwald's few survivors as hostages and marched them through Europe to a camp in Theresienstadt, north of Prague. Many died on the way. In early June, somebody who had returned from that Czechoslovakian camp told me Paul was there, alive. I didn't really believe it, but he came home around the middle of

Andy, age 2¹/₂,
when Paul came home
June 1945

June. Weighing only fifty kilograms—about 110 pounds—he was just skin and bones. It's hard to put my feelings into words. I was happy, grateful, and relieved. It was another miracle that the three of us were alive, along with my parents. Andy had a father. I celebrated.

"This is your daddy," I told Andy, who was standing on our little balcony, holding the rail.

Andy looked at him and said, "You are not my dad. My daddy's over there," pointing to a picture of Paul. Andy had bonded with that picture and had already gone through so many phases that this new person didn't mean anything. He saw him as an intruder rather than a friend. As Paul played and did things with him over the following weeks and months, Andy moved very, very slowly toward accepting him. Eventually, he got used to the idea that Paul was going to be living with us. For a long time, he wanted to be between us physically.

After the war, my Paris roommate Elsa Allan found me again through the U.S. embassy and sent all the papers for me to go to the United States. I still wanted to live in a free country, but Paul said he wasn't moving anywhere, because he was finally home. Never interested in politics, he didn't care whether we were going to live under communism or not, as long as it wasn't Nazism. So we stayed in Budapest and started a new life. I wrote Elsa back with my regrets. She knew about Andy from earlier correspondence, and she had sent us a huge parcel of chocolate. We appreciated that, and it also made us realize how little people elsewhere knew about how we were living and what we needed. In Hungary, it was a time when food was scarce and we had to stand in line for bread, which was rationed. Real food was valued. Chocolate was not really what we needed.

Paul had to regain weight and recuperate from his three-year ordeal. Then, not being a person who felt sorry for himself, he soon set up his veterinarian practice again. This time, he had his clinic at home. "I never look back," he declared, "I only look ahead." He was not angry at the Germans or about what had happened. The SS officer whose dog he'd treated had the nerve to ask Paul to testify for him. At Nuhrenberg and at smaller trials, those in charge of concentration camps could avoid prison only by getting prisoners to commend them. Paul was going to say yes, but I warned, "I'm not staying with you if you give any living Nazi any such support."

Feeling no need for revenge in his heart, Paul asked, "Am I going to be like them? Should we hang them all? That would just start something else." We didn't agree on this, because I was for revenge and felt very angry for a long, long time.

Two months after Paul came home, just as we began our life together, a telegram arrived from London. My former fiancé Jules was coming to get me at my parents' place. That's how we found out that he had never received the telegram I sent before my wedding. I felt mortified. He'd been transferred back to London from Turkey before it arrived.

When Jules arrived and phoned my parents, my father gave him our number, shaking, and told him I was married. Paul answered his call and invited him over for tea—a good English thing to do, he thought. When Jules arrived, we told him about everything: the secret police, the sudden halt in correspondence, and especially the telegram.

Eventually, he and Paul both agreed that I should choose between them. Paul said, "I took you away from him. We've hardly lived together." Clearly, he felt awful. Jules, having held on to our engagement, seemed more upset that I had broken my promise to him.

I had twenty-four hours to make my choice. Thinking long and hard, I walked the streets of Budapest. This was a major cross-road. If I wanted, I could finally go to London and live a good life there. Jules had a wonderful job at the Foreign Ministry. I had always wanted to get back to the west, and Paul didn't want to go. Also, Paul's generosity was such that we could stay good friends.

But I could not do that. I was firmly attached to Paul, and Andy was our son. I no longer had feelings for Jules. If I went with Jules, it would be acting out of guilt. That was very clear to me. So I phoned him and said I wanted to stay with Paul. It ended sadly.

All in all, the war years forced me to grow up, to stand on my own, to risk with courage, and to live with faith in the midst of despair, hate, cruelty, and disaster. My love for Andy saved me from giving up many times. I also believe that loving kept Paul and me alive.

Paul and Andy, 3
1946

Whatever you vividly
imagine, ardently desire,
sincerely believe and enthu-
siastically act upon . . . must
inevitably come to pass!
　　　　　—*George Shinn*

Growth means change and
change involves risks, stepping from the known to the
unknown.
　　　　　—*Soren Kierkegaard*

— 6 —

New Challenges and Choices

We had hoped that the Americans would liberate Hungary, but when our new life began after the war, our country was occupied—rather than liberated—by the Union of Soviet Socialist Republics. We didn't know what communism meant, but the propaganda said it was the opposite of Nazism. The communists promised freedom and equality for all. We would also be improving the lives of working people. I'm not saying that I became a communist, but I certainly wanted to work for a system that had these ideas. I believed in a better world. Many people, including Paul, never bought into that propaganda. To them, it was a joke, a lie.

In 1946, about a year after Paul came home, I started thinking about finding a job. I missed working. It was a very difficult choice, as Andy was only four and having difficulty settling into kindergarten. Whenever we left him, he screamed and cried. So each school we tried eventually discharged him. He wanted to stay at home, where he felt secure.

Paul and I decided to go to the lake for our first vacation. A famous psychologist had a beautiful kindergarten establishment in the mountains, and when we told him about Andy, he said, "Just bring me that kid. We will take him for a week." Two days later, we got a phone call to pick him up. The first day, he threw away the keys for his locker and his roommate's locker. Then he went to the outside gate and waited for the next two days. When we drove up and saw him, Paul asked, "What are you doing here?"

"I was waiting for you to come and take me home."

So we took him with us for the rest of our vacation. The second night, Paul and I explained to Andy that we were going out for a dance and that we would be back. At dinner, someone from the hotel found us in a restaurant and asked us to come back. Entering the lobby, we saw Andy sitting in his pajamas on the huge staircase and crying. The next day, the hotel asked us to leave.

Only much later did Andy agree to go to a nearby daycare place. Once he started school, he became independent, telling us, "I'm going to work now, like you do." From age six, he walked to school by himself and we never again had any of these problems.

Getting jobs was very easy after the war. The whole country was rebuilding. In 1946 and 1947, Hungary was climbing out of a disaster. We had been an agricultural country, but now there was no food. Buying bread meant standing in line for two hours. Even then, we were lucky if we did get bread or potatoes. Andy grew up on potatoes and beans, and some bread now and then. There was no milk. Sometimes we ate horsemeat, which was awful. It had to cook for hours before we could chew it. People in Budapest raised pigs in their bathtubs, to fatten them up either for Christmas or to have meat during the year. These became Paul's first patients. We kept a pig, too, but I didn't like having it in the bathtub and didn't feed it very well. I think it became depressed. So the vet's pig died.

The rate of inflation was horrible. If Paul made a *forint* in the morning, I had to run and buy gold or American dollars right away. Otherwise, the money would be worthless the next day. So life was interesting, and I didn't worry about politics. After all, we were all going to be equal.

When we woke up one morning at the end of 1947, we learned that the Socialist Party had become the Communist Party. It just changed color. Everybody who had been a member of the Socialist Party was now a member of the Communist Party. Suddenly, the country was moving from feudalism straight into socialism and communism. According to Marxist dogma, the normal process of growth would have involved going through capitalism first—but not so in Hungary.

New laws no longer allowed my father to practice at home as a lawyer. Fortunately, he was flexible enough to take on a legal job at a company. By 1948, Paul had reestablished his private veterinarian practice for pets. For a few years, he also taught veterinary medicine for the Hungarian army.

Budapest slowly got back on its feet. Years before, when the Communist Party had to operate underground, a sixteen-year-old boy named Vas Zoltán had been caught delivering messages to the Communist Party leader Rakosi Matyas. They both were arrested and sentenced to the most horrible prison for sixteen years. Then they were released to the Soviet Union in exchange for Hungarian flags held in Moscow since 1849. Both were heroes of the Communist idealists, and they remained in the USSR for the rest of the war. Then Rakosi resumed his role as Party leader in Hungary, while Zoltán returned to the starving city of Budapest and became its first postwar mayor. A fantastic administrator, he brought food to Budapest and became a much loved and important figure.

Zoltán's next job was to head the national bureau responsible for creating the new Communist system. One interesting rumor was that for his 120-person bureau, he hired professional

Zoltán
1982

people rather than members of the Party. Rather than being bu-
reaucratically minded, he made things happen. With one stroke,
he would give money or take it away. People grew afraid to walk
around the building that housed his agency. His organization was
like the Communist Party's right hand, and it set about nation-
alizing everything in Hungary: farms, land, and factories. Seen
as the Party's henchman, Zoltán had the kind of power that could
take away anybody's belongings in one second.

The Party confiscated villas and houses as well, and then
the Party or its leaders moved in. Many dispossessed landowners
moved into the little huts that had formerly housed their farm-
hands. In factories across the country, the authorities would walk
in and say, "Take your hat and your coat and leave. We're taking
over."

This had happened at the place where I had my first job, for instance. The factory's top man was a former worker, a man who was uneducated. Because I was university educated, I became his secretary and helped him run the factory. This was not my dream job. I wanted something more interesting. Fluent in several languages, I dreamed of a foreign ministry position that involved travel. Not being a Communist, however, I didn't have the right contacts.

One Sunday, Paul and I went with friends for a picnic in the mountains. As we enjoyed ourselves, a man came over and said hello to one of our friends, who invited him to sit down with us—and then introduced him as Zoltán. Taken aback, I took a minute or two to figure out that this friend worked for the government and thus knew Zoltán. While they spoke briefly, Andy was being his impossible six- or seven-year-old self. Watching him, Zoltán said, "This kid will either become a criminal or be brilliant. I don't know which, but he has terrible manners."

Meanwhile, my friend whispered to me, "If you want a job in the foreign ministry, tell him. He can do it."

Reputed to have a liking for beautiful women, Zoltán eyed my long red hair and asked, "Well, what do you do, little girl?"

"I work in a factory," I replied, "but I don't like it. I'm well educated, and I want to work in the foreign ministry."

"Little girl," he kept calling me that, "come to my office tomorrow, and maybe I can help you."

Not quite believing it, I thanked him. When Paul and I got home, we contemplated whether I should go. He didn't want me near that building: "You'll never get out of there again. We don't know what's going on in there."

But I was curious. The next day, to downplay my affluent middle-class background, I put on my darkest clothes and took the polish off my nails. Wearing no makeup, I went to see this big Communist leader. From behind his desk in a huge room, Zoltán studied me as I entered. "Don't you have a better coat? If you don't have the money for a better coat, I'll buy you one. That one is pretty shabby." He wanted to give me the message that this was not his kind of Communism. "Don't you wear nail polish?"

"Usually I do."

Having seen me the day before, he now saw through me right away. The conversation went on and, eventually, he asked, "What do you want to do?"

"I know several languages. I want to travel. I want a job in the foreign ministry."

"I'll look into it," he nodded. "Come back in two days."

Paul was waiting for me at an espresso cafe next door, ready to go in and save me unless I reappeared. Even when I told him the news, he was still worried: "Don't go back. It's not safe."

Returning to my job in the factory, I didn't tell my boss that I would miss work again in two days. When I went back, Zoltán said, "I've been thinking about it. I don't think I want you in the foreign ministry, but I want to give you a chance. Come and work with us here for six weeks. You'll be the first woman in the bureau. I want to show people that women are equal. You're an economist, and you'll fit in with the professional people here. If you prove yourself, you can stay. If not, I'll send you back to the factory. That's the deal."

I had no idea what kind of work they were doing, but it seemed like a challenge. It had to be better than working in the factory. Zoltán phoned my boss and told him I wouldn't be going back. My boss almost fainted because this man had called him directly.

When I told Paul about starting the next day, he was very upset. It was touch-and-go with us for a few days, but I was excited and curious about that bureau. Finally, I had work that challenged me. It soon turned into the most interesting job I've ever had. I started in the legal department, where everyone was working on proposing innovative laws, new ways to raise productivity, and new rules for living. No one knew how I had gotten my job (Zoltán said not to tell them anything), so they thought I had to be a Communist Party person. This department had created a lot of new laws already, but no one knew whether they were being implemented. My job was to look at the implementation of all the new regulations.

Everyone wanted to help me because they wanted to see whether their ideas and innovations were being carried out. For example, one chemical engineer had come up with the idea of using coal instead of wood in all the bakery ovens. Wood was in short supply. He showed me how to find out whether bakeries throughout Hungary were implementing this. He told me not to chase around for information, just to phone the minister of any area in question. Imagine suddenly being in a position to phone a minister and ask whether something had been implemented. I felt excited.

After the six weeks, I gave a report on a few matters, and Zoltán said I could stay. He also gave me a bonus for good work. This bureau eventually became the Planning Secretariat, which was responsible for planning everything. The secretariat was at the highest level of government and took its plans directly to the parliament. After plans were approved, the ministers had to implement them. The secretariat was above the ministries.

Advisors from the Soviet Union came and taught us the whole process of planning, from matters of the smallest store to the grandest projects. Again, however, Zoltán was not a bureaucrat. His was an administrator who did things without bureaucracy—and I liked that. I remained the only woman in the Planning Secretariat for a long time and was in charge of building a system for improving health, welfare, housing, and education in Hungary. I became very involved in my work because I believed in it. Zoltán did, too.

Hungary had ten counties, each with its own autonomous government. Dating from the old feudalistic structure, all of these were right-wing and still operated in that old way. Zoltán gave me the task of finding two or three people in each county whom we could trust, people who would implement the new system and regulations. They would be responsible directly to Zoltán. Without really knowing how to do this, I liked the idea of finding some good people and involving them in the work of the Planning Secretariat. Zoltán said, "Ask these people what they need in their area."

If they needed a nursing home, a bridge, or a road—anything that was in health, education, or housing—they would get it. He knew this would help persuade them of the benefits of the new political system, which rested on the principle of planning from the lowest local unit upward. That was the opposite of the feudalistic top–down process.

So I became responsible for setting up these smaller secretariats all over the country. To coordinate them and their work, I later became a department head. Zoltán had the greatest financial power in the country, so recruiting was fairly easy. Most people regarded the invitation to work for us as a great honor. The people I chose were really some of the best in the country, and I liked working with them. Later, almost all of them went on to become ministers or high-level bureaucrats.

Zoltán was a highly important influence in my life. I connected with him on the level of having the spirit to survive, to believe in and to fight for change. Working together, I learned how change and transformation can happen for a whole country. An idealist, he also had courage. He was brilliant, and I admired his humanism and ability to connect with people. From him, I learned administration and an organic view of the world. Administration is not limited by red tape. It is based on needs and providing resources to fulfill them. An organic view, in my mind, is based on the principles of freedom, respect, choices, self-responsibility, and humanness.

What I learned from Zoltán was a wonderful freelance way of administration, not the bureaucratic way. He approved money based on need, rather than rules. If money was needed for a purpose, he broke all the rules of the parliament and legislature. I learned that rules can and should be broken when necessary. This attitude often gets me into trouble now. Bureaucracy is everywhere, and I'm impatient when it gets in the way of helping people.

From 1949 to 1951, my first three years on this job, I really believed in planning. Housing, in short supply after the war, was one of my most important responsibilities. It was exciting to implement our five-year plans for a better life by building apartments, bridges, childcare facilities, and so on. In 1951, however, my statistics showed that housing had only improved by about 0.12 percent. The advisors said that the war in Korea and the situation in the Soviet Union didn't allow us to build more housing. I put this in my report. The next day's Party paper stated that our developmental rate as 125 percent instead of 0.12 percent. I told Zoltán, "There's a mistake in the paper."

Looking straight at me, he responded, "Do you want to live?"
"Yes."
"Do you want your family to live?"
"Yes."
"Then keep quiet."

In that moment, I realized everything was a lie. I had believed that I was contributing to Hungary's climb out of its postwar mess. What a ridiculous, naïve, and bizarre idea that was. Everything I worked for and believed in was not true. I was devastated.

I went to see all the other department heads, who said, "Are you crazy? Didn't you know that nothing is true?" I found out that the Central Party supervised each department in the secretariat. Everything we were doing in our plans was part of the big Soviet five-year plan, which was set in Moscow and not in our Planning Secretariat. So we were just puppets. We were producing things that the USSR needed for itself or one of its other puppet countries. Nothing had been built in Hungary, nothing had been taken care of. Our housing projects were not going ahead because what we needed went to Moscow.

Suddenly, it all seemed like a state of schizophrenia. I had worked day and night. I had neglected Andy and Paul to sort out these statistics, only to realize that everything was a lie. The Party was taking our figures and changing them. There was only one newspaper, the Party paper, and the people there wrote whatever they wanted. They were all lies, but now I felt responsible for the propaganda. This whole system led by Soviet advisers was full of lies. The ideas they advertised were not practiced. People were not free, and the plans never materialized during that Stalinist era. I became very skeptical after that day. It ended my idealistic belief in the future of my country. I felt disappointed, stressed, and sick.

One day, I fainted in the office. People there sent me by ambulance to the so-called Party hospital. Admission there was considered an honor, as that hospital had the specialists, equipment, and antibiotics that were not available for other people. They also had a particular program imported from the Soviet Union. When authorities wanted to get rid of some important Party official, they assigned that tired or exhausted person to this so-called sleep therapy. Unfortunately, some never woke up.

After fainting, I came to in a hospital room with a few women who were all sleeping. I was terrified. Because I was an interesting case—I had had meningitis a few years before, when Andy was two—I became a guinea pig. The doctors drained my spinal fluid many times. I could not walk, and I had terrible headache all the time. They did not let anybody visit me. It felt like being in jail, and I sensed the danger. I knew I wasn't important enough for the Party to get rid of, but also not important enough to receive proper treatment. My spinal fluid was leaking. I could feel the wetness under my back.

One night, I gathered all my energy and crawled to a phone and called a friend who was a pathologist. I knew the Party hospital was terrified of pathologists because they knew the truth: that some people were killed in some medical places. My friend came to my bedside and asked what I wanted. I said I wanted to go to the neurological clinic. He said I had the right to be discharged, so a nurse took me to an office nearby, where many physicians and nurses stood, staring at me. They said that if I stayed, I would get antibiotics; if I didn't, I wouldn't. It felt like tribunal, a court case. So much for my experience in the country's best hospital.

Very weak and tired, I discharged myself. By the time my friend got me to the clinic, I was too weak to stand. I remember lying down on the street while he went in to get me a bed. Once admitted, a decent physician took over my treatment. He said they had taken so much fluid from my spine that it would take a while to recover.

All these experiences woke me up from my dream about working for my country, believing the propaganda, and believing that I could do anything. During the war, I had learned about the horrors of Nazism. Now I experienced the equal horrors of communism. Crushed and disappointed, I also knew that I was stuck. The government and the Party decided where people should work. So, until the Party entrusted someone else with my job, I was a prisoner. I became an enemy of the system. Yet, to survive, I had to work for the system. Rebelling, I decided to work underground—a very dangerous situation. Those of us who did this had to be careful, of course. We were all watched. Some of the people in my own department were watching all my phone calls and all my moves. People who were not cautious enough ended up in jail. Some of our friends who were good people were imprisoned. Sometimes we didn't know what was wrong with us, that the system retained us rather than putting us in jail, too. Living that kind of underground resistance was very dangerous and painful.

Andy had to learn a double system of thinking. Paul and I trusted him to the degree that we were saying, "Don't tell anybody in the school that we are listening to the BBC" (the outlawed British Broadcasting Corporation radio). It was just like the Nazi system: very often, kids started to talk and the parents ended up in jail. But we wanted Andy to know that we didn't believe in what was going on all around us. I also told him, "Don't believe what they are telling you about Stalin, about the Russians, about Communism. Don't believe it. We don't believe in that." it was very difficult to live that way.

By 1951, Hungary was under Stalinist leaders appinted by the Communist Party. Suddenly, they began dismissing any of their own people whose Stalinist loyalty was in doubt. At an April meeting of our department heads one day, a high Party official announced that Zoltán would no longer be the chairperson because he had made some mistakes that the Party could not tolerate.

The real story was that they did not trust him any more. He was too liberal and too idealistic, too honest and too good. He no longer agreed with what was going on in the Party. They also held it against him that he had helped his sister go to Israel, and she never came back. The Party was suspicious of him because he was truly humane. He had no blood on his hands. Earlier, when he nation-alized factories, he had let people leave the country with money. This was now also held against him.

Zoltán represented the value of believing that change can happen and life can be better. His downfall was that he believed in the idealistic principles of Marxism but worked for a Party system that eventually betrayed those principles in practice. He hated dictatorship, just as I hated it, and he wasn't dictatorial enough for the Communist system. He had the courage and determination to stand up against the whole Party. They dismissed him because he didn't agree with the methods of Stalinism.

He was one of the founders of the Hungarian Communist Party—and one of its many victims, as well. This is an example of what happened at the highest Party level. A saying at the time was: "The Party eats up its own people." However, Zoltán never felt like a victim. Later in his life, someone asked, "Did you ever leave the Party?" He answered, "No, the Party left me a long time ago."

Zoltán lost everything and was reassigned to work in a mine in the southern part of Hungary. Anyone who had worked with or been associated with him also fell under suspicion. My telephone was tapped, and I was watched. In those days, the secret police were detaining, imprisoning, and torturing people. Sometimes, they simply killed them. That was how the worst of Stalinism was introduced to and practiced in Hungary.

A few weeks after Zoltán's dismissal, I got a message from the mother of his secretary, Edith. Zoltán and Edith had fallen in love when he was mayor of Budapest. Unfortunately, he had a Russian wife, whom he had married while in the Soviet Union. As the Communist Party would not agree to their divorce, he couldn't end the marriage to marry Edith. With the Party being against them, Zoltán and Edith were in kind of a Romeo and Juliet story, living together in a deeply loving relationship. She was a wonderful woman, and we were good friends.

Edith's mother did not dare to come to my office or home, so we met in a local park. She told me Edith was being tortured. The police wanted her to sign a paper denouncing Zoltán. Edith somehow got a note out, telling her mother to let me know this and for me to let Zoltán know what was happening to her. If they continued her torture for another twenty-four hours, she would sign anything. She was very honest about it. She had her limits, and she was not going to submit to any further torture. From the room she was in, she heard people being tortured and screaming. Then the police made a hole in the wall and made Edith watch as a torturer cut off another woman's breast. The police threatened Edith, "We are going to do that with you if you don't sign that paper."

It was crucial to get the information to Zoltán. He might still have enough influence to free her. So, while I knew that the secret police were watching everybody and everything, I took the risk. Paul was totally against my driving down to see Zoltán, of course, but I felt strongly that I had to face the danger.

The next day was May 1, when everyone in the Communist system would be marching in the streets to celebrate Labor Day. My job benefits included having the use of a car and a chauffeur. The chauffeur liked me and adored Zoltán, so he was willing to take the risk as well. We drove south 200 miles to where Zoltán was working in a mine. With great difficulty, I got someone to find him. This man, who had been in charge of the country's entire economy, now sat in a small room. I saw a tiger in a cage.

When I told him about Edith, he didn't believe me. At the time of his humiliating dismissal, he had gotten assurances of her safety from the leader of the Party, the same man with whom he had been in jail for sixteen years. Nothing was going to happen to Edith—that was Zoltán's condition for agreeing to go to the mines.

"Do you really believe that I'd risk coming down here otherwise?" I asked. He knew what I meant. Not trusting anybody, the Party's "building spies" had been watching all of us in the Secretariat after Zoltán's dismissal. So he began to come around. Eventually, he phoned the Party leader, who washed his hands of responsibility, saying, "Oh, it's probably the Minister of Internal Affairs." He soon called back, confirming that Edith was with the secret police. Zoltán got his assurance that she would be released.

When the Party leader asked how Zoltán knew about Edith's situation, he replied, "I know. I just know." So now Zoltán asked, "Little girl, how will you get back now?"

"I'm not sure." We had to take precautions, as secret police were all over the place. Zoltán told my chauffeur to go visit his grandmother in the eastern part of Hungary. He told me to fly back to Budapest.

Once I was in the Budapest airport, I was scared and nervous about anybody walking behind me. I did not believe I'd get away with this. I phoned Edith's mother, who said that Edith was home. She was in the shower, and she was drinking and crying, saying that she couldn't trust Zoltán any more, since he'd allowed this to happen. Her mother told me not to come over, as secret police were sitting in front, watching who was going in and out of the house. They were looking for any possible connection between Edith and Zoltán.

The Party dismissed Edith from her job as persona non grata and sent her to live in eastern Hungary, out of the way. Her mother went with her. Each day, Edith had to go to the local police station to prove that she was still there. In Budapest, things turned really bad. From one day to the next, I was never sure whether I would have my job, my freedom, or even my life. The Party had assigned one of their women to watch me and to listen in on my tapped calls. Everyone in the Secretariat knew by then that I was not a trustworthy worker for the political system. I had to learn new ways to survive.

The planning process became a monster. We had to submit five-year plans for everything from the smallest corner grocery to the country's largest hospitals. Honest people suffered under this system, which truly limited efficiency and creativity. For example, the wonderful pediatrician who had saved Andy's life found me in my office one day. He explained that he was facing an impossible task: "How on earth can I know how many nurses and how much medicine I'll need five years from now?"

One good outcome of having my job was that I could repay this doctor in a way that saved his sanity and probably many lives. I told him that as long as I was in my position, his children's hospital would get everything it needed. This was the least I could do for him and for all the children in that hospital. God works in many ways.

In 1954, my father was hospitalized for a few days for minor surgery to correct a very mild prostate condition. It was the first time in his life that he was sick, let alone hospitalized. Knowing that he was scared, I visited him every day. The day before the surgery, I had a horrible premonition of seeing him dead in his bed. When I told Paul, he thought I was too concerned, since the operation was going to be minor. That day, when I saw him, my father asked me to give his sister a certain amount of money (and not to tell my mother).

The next morning, June 7, 1954, I went to see him before his surgery. I just knew how terrified he was. When I got to his hospital room, I found his bed stripped. His roommate told me that my father had had a perfect angiogram in the morning. Then, around breakfast time, he had a heart attack and died.

I know he died from the fear of surgery. He'd never had any heart trouble until then. It was the first time that I experienced the loss of a loved one—and I loved him so much. I felt alone and thought nobody would ever love me as much. I did not know how to survive without him, even though I had Andy and Paul to support me. My mother told me, "I am sorry for you. I should be the one who is dead, because you loved him so much." At that moment, I made the commitment to take care of her as long as she lived.

Me at age 36
1956

My father's
gravestone

Our last summer in Hungary
1956

Life begins on the other side
of despair.
—Jean Paul Sartre

— 7 —

The Revolution

In 1953, after Joseph Stalin's death, Nikita Khrushchev came
to power in the Soviet Union. He opened the door a little by
allowing criticism within the Party. This may have been a mistake, from his point of view, because a dictatorial regime cannot
open that door at all. People soon began to criticize the Party.
They expressed their outrage at various situations. For example,
if a worker took ten cents' worth of something from a factory, he
would be sent to jail. Such harsh sentencing came under much
discussion. And as they thought and spoke about such things,
people became more and more outraged at authoritarian and
cavalier practices.

In every satellite communist country, for instance, the Soviets
had fabricated the same sham accusations and trials of high-
ranking officials. In Hungary, these false charges were brought
against Rajk László, the Minister of Internal Affairs (former
Minister of Foreign Affairs). All over the radio and newspapers,
we heard people testifying against him, but we didn't believe
them. We knew it was just made-up propaganda.

For example, a friend of mine disappeared one day. A
housewife, she was not political. When her husband tried to find
her, he was advised not to get involved unless he wanted to
disappear as well. Then we heard her on the radio, testifying as a

witness in this trial. We knew she had nothing to do with it. When she was liberated from jail, we showed her the documentation of the trial, including her testimony. It was a surprise to her. Visiting her parents once, she explained, she'd simply happened to witness a meeting between this minister and a high-ranking official from another country. It was being at the wrong place at the wrong time that led to her arrest and testimony.

The Hungarian minister was convicted and hanged as a traitor to the Party and to the system. Knowing he was innocent, his wife made so much noise that this trial became a widely discussed issue. Eventually, the Party leader in Hungary declared that they had made a mistake, the minister had been innocent. His wife demanded and got a state funeral for her husband.

This episode symbolized the political injustice of that time. Until that state funeral, the silent rage and despair of the people in Budapest threatened to boil over. It was not enough, obviously, that the Party leaders said, "Sorry, we made a mistake." People were still being jailed for small crimes or for no reason at all. Our awareness of injustice grew on all levels, and I believe this contributed to the consciousness that eventually led to the Hungarian revolution on October 23, 1956.

University students and the working class, in particular, became active. So did the intellectuals, of course, who had their own newspaper. More and more dirty, horrible stories came out. The government grew more liberal and brought back Zoltán, who became a Minister of Economy and Agriculture. A born optimist, he predicted, "Things are going to change."

At all levels—from people in the army to intellectuals to the general population—Hungarians became increasingly aware that the Party continued to lie and that we lived under its oppression. For example, we had no food because of the Korean war. We realized that we were just satellites, supporting the big Soviet system. The Party's lies and inconsistencies led to more and more distress, distrust, unhappiness, and outrage.

I still had my position in the Planning Secretariat, but I wasn't into it any longer. I was just treading water, waiting to see whether change would come. Sitting in my office on October 23, 1956, I heard that students from the university were marching to demand that the Party concede twelve points. These included fundamental freedoms, such as freedom of speech and freedom for the press. The students assembled peacefully at the square with the statue of Petôfi Sándor, a hero of our 1849 revolution and one of our greatest poets, whose works focus on freedom and fighting for freedom.

The response of Party leaders was "No." They directed the students to go home. But the demonstrations continued. Students marched all over the city. As people heard what was going on, they joined the march. I went over to Zoltán's office to find out what he thought would happen. Very hopeful, he said, "The big change is happening. Let's join them."

We walked through the streets of Budapest toward the Party building, which was on a big square where more and more people were gathering. Anger, frustration, and hope filled the air. By late afternoon, a huge crowd stood in front of the Party building, demanding the twelve freedom points. In a moment, everything changed. Someone shouted, "Fire on the students." From the building, secret police shot into the crowd. The students were not armed. Many fell wounded or dead. Later, people from all the factories around Budapest arrived in trucks with weapons they had gotten from the military. Soldiers also joined the protest on October 23, 1956. The revolution was on.

*During the
Hungarian
Revolution
October 1956*

The army, the working class, and students fought the secret police. What started in a peaceful way became a violent revolution. It was not directed or instigated by the west, as Soviet propaganda later suggested, although the ongoing promises of Radio Free Europe did encourage us to act. Many people died. That evening, we learned that the Party leaders had fled by helicopter to the Soviet Union. The crowd soon marched to the square of the parliament building. There, our newly elected premier, Nagy Imre, declared that he was forming a socialist government, that the revolution was against the oppression of the Soviet dictatorship, and that Hungary wanted freedom from the Soviet Union. He wanted peace and collaboration with east and west.

Euphoric, we believed that we would finally have freedom. We had won in this impossible David and Goliath situation. The next few days were full of euphoria and, at the same time, tremendous chaos. People were hanging secret police all over town and throwing open the jails.

The day after the revolt, the Soviet Union recalled military troops that had been stationed in Hungary since 1945, as a result of the World War II peace treaties. Having been in Hungary for eleven years, those soldiers had become friends of the people. They would not fight us. Nonetheless, Budapest's residents lined the biggest avenue—ironically enough, Stalin Boulevard—and celebrated the departure of the Soviet military. Crowds demolished statues of Stalin and carried the pieces through the streets. Communist literature was burning all over the city. As we found out later, Soviet politicians recalled these troops to keep their people from knowing that we had staged a rebellion against Soviet communism.

These were great moments, the first time I felt proud to be Hungarian. In our country's history of turmoil, Hungarians had always operated against each other. Now, a single consciousness and connection between people came into being. We united against oppression. I again believed that everything would change.

In those days, government officials worked in the parliament building. Because of the chaos in the city following the revolution, their families also moved in and lived in that building. During my frequent visits there to see Edith and Zoltán, I realized that the government was not aware of how much chaos existed throughout Budapest. They were planning to create order, but first they focused on negotiating peace with the Soviet Union. Then, at a meeting between the two governments during the first week of November, the new Hungarian Minister of Defense was shot.

At 4 A.M. on November 4, Soviet troops invaded Hungary via Czechoslovakia. Four thousand tanks invaded Budapest, which was without arms. At 5 o'clock in the morning, Premier

Nagy Imre went on the radio to ask for help from the west. He repeated his urgent message in twelve languages.

When I woke up to find a tank parked in front of my apartment building, I phoned my mother and my friends to say goodbye. The first thought for each of us was that we would die. We did not know what had happened to our new government and our dreams of freedom.

People fought back as best they could. The only way to fight the tanks was with Molotov cocktails. From the rooftops, teenage boys threw bottles containing homemade explosive liquids onto the tanks. It worked, but the more tanks they blew up, the more horrible the retaliation became. Around the end of November, the Soviet army swept city streets to kidnap boys between ten and eighteen. That was the age group responsible for throwing the homemade bombs. No one ever saw them again. Paul and I knew we had to get Andy, then thirteen, out of the country.

As the fighting went on in Budapest, what we experienced was total betrayal, fear, anger, and hopelessness. Our government officials and their families had all disappeared from the parliament building, and we did not know what had happened to them. We feared the worst.

We couldn't walk on the streets without a tank following us. With less and less food in the markets, we had more and more fear—and no solutions to the Soviet invasion. By the middle of November, when the fighting stopped, the Soviet tanks and military had won.

The Soviets set up a puppet Hungarian government, which began restoring order. Coming out of their tanks, the first thing the Soviet soldiers asked was where the ocean was. We were surprised because Budapest is far from the ocean. It turned out that

Poster sent
from
Hungary
1956

these troops did not know they were in Hungary. They couldn't read our alphabet, and their officers had told them they were fighting the British in the Suez Canal, where a conflict raged at the time. This confirmed that our revolution was a secret in the Soviet Union.

Among ourselves, we heard that Hungarian freedom fighters had removed the land mines at the border with Austria. That border was part of the Iron Curtain. With the land mines gone, it was now possible to escape the country. That—and the utter chaos everywhere—created our first opportunity in eleven years to leave Hungary. Before the revolution, getting out had been hopeless. I had always wanted at least to get my son out somehow.

———◆◆◆◆———

By 1956, Andy was thirteen and ready to go to high school. However, even though I was responsible for the whole country's educational system, I couldn't get him into any school. Under communism, high schools and universities admitted only the children of families in the working class and peasant class. Paul and I were professionals, as were our fathers, so Andy was excluded. Not wanting to raise him in that system, and knowing he was still at high risk for being kidnapped off the streets, I had no doubts about leaving the country at the first opportunity. In addition, I was convinced that I would rather die than live under this Soviet system any longer.

When Paul and I decided to stay in Budapest after World War II, I had had high hopes for freedom, for the values the Socialists announced, and for a better world. Then, under the Communist regime, we couldn't leave. Now, I knew that if we stayed, I would not be able to look myself in the face. I would commit spiritual suicide. Leaving meant abandoning all our belongings, risking the real dangers of an illegal exit, going into the unknown, and not being allowed back into our country again. But no matter the danger, we decided to go. In a way, we had made the decision long before, and now our opportunity had arrived.

Again, escape was dangerous. The Russians shot the people they caught or shipped them to Siberia. Escape was also too difficult physically for an older person, so we would have to go without my mother and everything we owned. I probably could never have left if my father had still been alive, because he would not have been able to come along, either. However, my mother encouraged me to leave. I promised her that I would do everything to make it possible to join us later.

Even the three of us could not go as a family. That would be too suspicious. For me, leaving the country was even more dangerous than for Paul, because he'd never had anything to do with politics. All the same, we decided to risk going into the unknown. People often think that was courage, but it came out of absolute desperation. We would rather die than stay.

The Soviets had set up checkpoints every ten kilometers between Budapest and the Austrian border. Moving from village to village toward the west would require false identification papers and cover stories. In a communist country, officials check these everywhere you go, and no one is a person without them. People often made false papers from potatoes. Paul was the administrator of a plant that bred and trained German shepherds for the police, so he made up papers showing that he was traveling near the border to buy some animals. Andy's false papers said that he was Paul's kennel boy, named Kovacs. They would go in Paul's government car. His chauffeur, Steve, was a newly wed young man who had been an engineer but lost his license after being caught leaving the country five years before. He had to leave his bride behind.

The three of them left around November 20. Agreeing to meet in London if we made it, Paul and I memorized the phone number of his sister who lived there. We didn't dare carry it with us. Dressing Andy in two pairs of socks and two of every other piece of underwear, I told him I would do everything possible to get out and to meet them. We got little news about the border, so I did not know how I would make it. If I didn't, I wanted him to know that I loved him and that I had tried.

When they left, my heart broke. It was one of the hardest times in my life. I cried for days, not knowing whether I would ever see them again. Yet, I also knew that if anyone could make it, Paul would. Andy was in the best possible hands.

To make things look normal, I still had to go to the office every day. Most of the people I knew wanted to leave the country, and we talked whenever possible about getting a group together and getting a vehicle. My office phone was tapped, and I was surrounded by people I didn't trust, so it was difficult to make connections. It also became increasingly hard to join a group as a woman alone.

One day, my mother told me she'd had a call from Steve, the chauffeur that left with Paul. After getting to Austria safely, they had waited in a border village, hoping to meet Steve's wife and me when we got out of Hungary. She and I had hoped to go together, but we never found a group to go with. So, after waiting several days, Steve crossed back and returned to Budapest for his young bride. It was a huge risk—of both his life and his newly gained freedom. For me, it was another miracle. No one else would return after making that dangerous escape. And going back to the border with his wife would be another huge risk.

He was getting together a group of ten people who wanted to leave. I got in touch with him as soon as I could, and he told me that Paul and Andy were alive and had made it across the border. What a relief that was.

Steve found a truck that would get the ten of us to the border, and we made our false papers. We each made about ten different pieces of identification, saying that we lived in a different place between Budapest and the border. Our story was that we were buying food and potatoes in the next village.

Our group left ten days after Paul and Andy went. We women all dressed like peasants, wearing babushkas. I wore my worst clothes and took a beach bag—no money, no passport, no jewelry, not even a toothbrush. For a while, we rode in the back of the truck through the cold December countryside. Luckily, the authorities who stopped us and asked for our papers were all Russians. They didn't know what real Hungarian identification papers looked like. At every checkpoint, I died a hundred deaths until they said, "*Harasho*" (okay) and "*Davai*" (you can go).

Near the Austrian border, we left the truck. By then, it was dark. The biggest problem now was ahead. Some of the mines were still in the ground near the border, we had heard, and many people had died from stepping on them. Because the border did not run in a straight line and was not marked, we would not be able to tell which way to go. Sometimes people lost their children and got turned around or went back to Hungary by mistake.

Ahead, we saw lights of the border police, who were shooting from a tower at people trying to cross. Steve, who had once been a soldier, suggested that we follow the nearby railroad track toward Austria. We did. Whenever we saw lights moving toward us from the border police, we rolled down the snowy banks of the track so they couldn't see us.

For what seemed like hours, I walked in sheer terror. At one point, I really wanted to give up. I was afraid the police would shoot me in the leg, leaving me unable to move. That was the most awful thing I could imagine. They would probably send me to Siberia. Again, at that moment, I was not afraid to die; but I did not want to lose my past and my future, either. I went on.

We realized we were in Austria only when we saw our first Austrian soldier. That man got more hugs than he probably ever had had in his life. Soon, we were at one of the wonderful International Red Cross stations set up to take care of Hungarian refugees. They offered us food and shelter at a nearby camp, and would later fly us wherever we wanted to go. Not wanting to be restricted in my freedom, which I had just gained, I wasn't about to go to a camp for Hungarians. Since all our jails had been thrown open during the revolution, Nazis, communists, and criminals alike were also leaving the country and passing themselves off as freedom fighters. I didn't want to be around them. Instead, I wanted to go to Vienna to find Paul and Andy. That was all I cared about.

Since I spoke fluent German, I got myself on a train and went to Vienna, where I asked at a police station if I could call a relative in England. When they said yes, I called Paul's sister at the number I had memorized. That's how I learned that Andy and Paul were on their way to London.

Until then, we'd had no way to communicate. If Paul had called me in Budapest to say he and Andy were safe, it would have incriminated me. The authorities would have held me hostage to force them to return. Radio Free Europe promised to forward coded messages from refugees to those they left behind, but Paul's message had never reached me. And now, he and Andy did not know that I was in Austria.

Even so, no words can describe how I felt that first day in Vienna. I remember walking along the streets, where people gave us refugees free coffee and free bus rides. I was alive, in the West, and very happy. I just knew that Paul, Andy, and I would make it in this part of the world, because we were all alive. Traditional values—such as money and security—all changed for me. I had nothing and I had everything because I was free. I decided never to buy or own anything again. One is free when one doesn't own things.* It was the greatest day of my life.

---

* I still believe this, yet when I look around my beautiful home now, I realize that over the years, I have again collected too many things.

To avoid the organized refugee camps, I happily spent the night at the police station. The next day, I again wandered along Vienna's streets. Ironically, the only person I met was a former girlfriend of Paul, who gave me shelter for the night. She had also met Paul and Andy before they left for London, so I had news about them.

Another irony was calling Stephen, one of the cousins who had kept me prisoner as a child. Now living in England, he offered to send me money and a visa via the British embassy in Vienna. When I went there, however, I couldn't get near the door because thousands of Hungarians were standing in a queue.

The Red Cross was fantastic in handling the 200,000 Hungarians who were crossing into Austria. None of us had passports or any identification, but they didn't insist on bureaucracy. They simply gave priority to people who had nowhere to go in Europe, no relatives waiting. The Red Cross immediately shipped such people to a country of their choice. So, for example, Steve and his wife were in Toronto a few days after we came across the border.

As I waited my turn to get into the embassy, British officials asked me the purpose of my waiting. Then they took me out of the line and put me in a bus, took me to the airport, and sent me to London—again, without money, a visa, or any identification. This was like magic to me.

Government people at the London airport were more organized and insisted that refugees receive identification papers before being set loose. They explained that I could make one phone call, to Paul's English brother-in-law, and they would release me into his hands only. Then, when they learned that he was two hours from the airport, they decided instead to put me on a bus to an old military camp in Scotland that was now a camp for Hungarian refugees. So there I was, finally on British soil, and I ended up with tons of Hungarians, most of whom I was suspicious about.

The next day, I noticed that only one policeman was in charge of issuing identification papers to the refugees. At that rate, I figured it would take me weeks to get out. So I asked him to let me phone my cousin. Stephen was surprised to hear where I was, because the British embassy in Vienna kept telling him that I never reached them. Obviously, the left hand didn't know what the right was doing. After my call, Stephen arranged a police escort for me to get back to London, where I finally saw Andy and Paul. My joy about being together was fuller than it had ever been.

In addition, Paul's two sisters and their families were there. Elisabeth, the younger sister, had survived her ordeals in Auschwitz, but their mother had been killed there. So our joy was mixed with grief. Later, we also saw the cousins of mine who lived in England.

During Paul and Andy's escape from Hungary, things had gone less than smoothly than Steve had told me. Although Paul and I had taught Andy not to call Paul "Daddy" while they were traveling to the border, he had slipped once after they picked up a Hungarian hitchhiker. Paul kicked him, and nothing bad ended up happening. The next day, they drove toward a footbridge that would take them across the border, but it was a trap. Russian soldiers had blown it up that morning, and they now surrounded the car.

They took Paul, Andy, and Steve to a prison camp for people suspected of fleeing the country. Steve swallowed a document he carried that proved he had once wanted to leave for the West. When they got there, Paul told a Russian officer, "How dare you stop me from going to buy something for my government?" He had such self-determination that he was trying to bluff his way out. After a few hours at the camp, however, they were loaded onto a truck that probably would have taken them to a prison camp. Fortunately, all three of them managed to escape from the truck somehow. They all ran in different directions, eventually making their way back to a local town. There, a Hungarian policeman who'd been helping refugees got them across the border into Austria.

Now, in London for the first time, we had nothing but freedom and choices. Paul and I had left everything to walk into the unknown, the unpredictable. We did not know where we would end up. We were all lucky: we got out. And we had the courage and faith to go on. Although we had no money or jobs, we were in the free world, where I had wanted to be since I was young. I had my husband and my son again, and I was overjoyed.

The greatest discovery of
any generation is that
human beings can alter
their lives by altering the
attitudes of their minds.

—*Albert Schweitzer*

If there is a sin against life,
it consists perhaps not so
much in despairing of life as
in hoping for another life
and eluding the implacable
grandeur of this life.

—*Albert Camus*

To dare is to lose one's
footing momentarily. To not
dare is to lose oneself.

—*Soren Kierkegaard*

— *8* —

Risks and Courage

As refugees in London, we had choices about where we wanted to emigrate. Ever since my days in Paris, I had always wanted to go to California. Now was my big chance to live by the ocean in a warm place. Paul and I went to the U.S. embassy, where I found myself asking, "Do you have mandatory military service or the draft?" Somehow, this question came out of my mouth immediately. My only absolute bias about moving anywhere was that, if I could help it, Andy was never going to wear a soldier's uniform.

The embassy official said, "Yes, he would be drafted at age eighteen." My dream about California went down the drain. (As we found out later, if we had gone to the United States, Andy would have been drafted for the war in Vietnam.)

"Which country does not have compulsory military service?" When he said, "Jamaica and Canada," we went to the Canadian embassy. There, still wanting to live by the ocean, we asked to go to Vancouver. Our names went on a waiting list because the Red Cross's first priority then was to ship the 200,000 Hungarian refugees then in Austria. Canada was allowing in 37,000 refugees, but we would have to wait a few months.

Waiting was no problem, as both Paul and I had relatives in England. When I reconnected with my cousins, they did not remember any part of abusing me. As adults, they wanted to be connected and to help; and they couldn't believe I had been terrified as a child. Having moved to England in 1938, they were all well established by then. They offered us many room-and-board arrangements, including a house on the beach. Their unexpected support and love was overwhelming for me. I just wanted to be on my own with my family. Also guiding me, I think, was my spirit for not being dependent on relatives—Paul's or mine.

I saw my friend Steven again for the first time since I left Paris. We had lost touch when World War II suspended the mail between England and Hungary. Now I learned that he had been drafted, ended up in India, and contracted polio. For many years, this restricted him from walking and living independently. When I saw him in December 1956, he could drive again, in a special car. With the help of orthopedic devices, he was walking again, too. I was amazed at what he did with his will power to survive and function.

It was beautiful to reconnect with him and to share our stories. We were very interested in each other's experiences. Since our days in France, we had lived in very different worlds and survived very different challenges. His life sort of stopped in Dieppe, where we often met while I lived in Paris, and he romanticized our relationship for a long time. Meanwhile, my life was full of events, so we grew in different directions. Nonetheless, our respect and love for each other endures.*

Our first Christmas in the west was an experience. For example, we were shocked that people celebrated in the morning,

* Today, Steven is in his nineties, lives alone, and looks after himself. He never had his own family. From talking over our great memories whenever I'm in London, I know he's never lost his idealism.

wearing pajamas for breakfast. In Hungary, we celebrated on Christmas Eve, dressed up. Before midnight, the angels would bring the tree for the kids. In London, Andy found money hidden in his pudding, and that was odd as well for us.

While we stayed for a few weeks with my sister-in-law, we put an ad in the *London Times*. It said that a Hungarian veterinarian and his family wanted to work while awaiting emigration to Canada. Jobs were almost impossible to get in London. In addition, Paul and Andy didn't know English, and I knew only some. The first person who responded to the ad was Jules, my former fiancé, who asked my sister-in-law whether the ad was about Paul. He wanted to see Paul, and he offered to help if he needed anything. He worked in the Foreign Office. For the next few months, he insisted on meeting Paul regularly and teaching him English. Paul went out of guilt. Sometimes, he took Andy with him. One day, he told Jules, "Maria is here, too, you know."

As if he had waited for this moment, Jules replied, "Who?" I got the message: to Jules, I did not exist. Paul felt embarrassed. There he was again, caught in the middle. Nonetheless, he was polite and kept his relationship with Jules. I felt both angry and curious to see Jules, but I let Paul's relationship with him be the end of that story.

Me with Steven
1990

The next person who called about the ad was Alex, an English gentleman who lived thirty miles outside London in Hatfield Broad Oak, near Bishop's Stortford. Needing a housekeeper, he was interested in having a Hungarian refugee family as temporary help until he filled the job with someone permanent. As soon as he said the house had central heating and hot water (which was rare then in England), I agreed to meet him about the job. I knew nothing about housekeeping, of course, especially English housekeeping. In Hungary, we had maids who did everything from shopping to babysitting. I knew how to cook only a couple of Hungarian dishes, and I knew even less about English food. I had never even seen a toaster.

Complete with bowler hat and folded umbrella, Alex came to see us in London. He was a decent looking man of about sev-

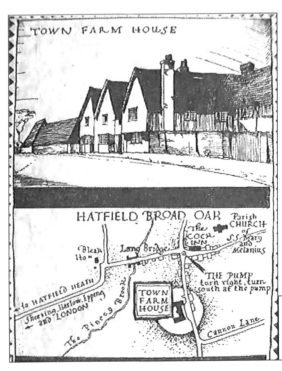

Hatfield Broad Oak, England 1957

enty, and Paul and I soon agreed to the arrangement. Most of all, we both wanted to be on our own instead of with relatives. Alex said he'd take us to his house that day. When he suggested we bring our luggage, we laughed. We had none. So he drove us out from London to his town, where rich people lived in very elegant old houses. Like Alex, many of these people's daily routine was to commute to London by train.

Rather than the housekeeper's quarters, Alex offered us the guest quarters. This consisted of two bedrooms, a bathroom, and a separate toilet. Taking us around the rest of his house, it was clear that he was very proud that it was 500 years old and full of antiques. I couldn't have cared less. What got my attention was the kitchen, which was the size of a whole apartment in Budapest and had a huge, terrifying stove.

Being a housekeeper was going to be a real challenge. My role was to cook. Paul's was to take care of the boilers for the heating and hot water system, which he didn't know anything about until Alex showed him how to feed them. Paul told me to listen carefully, as he didn't understand one word. As Alex explained about the hot water system, the heating system, and the stove, I struggled to take it all in. Unfortunately, I didn't understand much more than Paul.

The first night, Alex said he wanted an English breakfast— tea and eggs and toast—the next morning. I had a sleepless night, wondering how to do all those things at the same time. I got up at 6 A.M. and made the tea, then the toast, and then the eggs. It took me a long time, and it was no surprise that Alex didn't eat any of it. It was cold by the time he came down. He left without food, and I was devastated. I felt stupid and angry about not being able to do this simple task.

By then, it was time to tend to the boilers. Trying to remember what Alex had said, I told Paul to feed them as much as he could. I had to plan dinner. Nervous after the breakfast disaster, I decided on veal. Schnitzel was something I did know how to cook. At noon, a woman named Mrs. Carr came to do the shopping. She took me with her to the butcher, but she insisted on steak because veal was the most expensive meat in England. (Later, I found out that the whole village was gossiping about Alex's new housekeeper, who was so extravagant that she wanted to buy veal.) Not wanting to admit that I didn't know how to cook steak, I asked, "How do you make beef?" She told me to cook it three minutes on one side, and three on the other. I had never heard of anything like this. In Hungary, we never heard of steak, but we cooked beef in a sauce for hours and hours.

Meanwhile, Paul was still feeding fuel into the boilers. By the time Mrs. Carr and I got back, the boilers were choked and everything stopped. The stove still worked, though, so I started feeding it and cooking the steak. By the time Alex came home, the house had grown cold, and we had no hot water. The stove had also been overfilled and wouldn't work either, even to make tea. The steak, which had cooked for hours before the stove stopped, was as tough as a shoe. In despair, I knew I had failed.

Alex said, "Don't worry about anything. Let's have a drink." Paul loved that. Soon we were all sitting in his nice living room with a warm fireplace. W1e had no food for dinner, but Alex again told us not to worry. "Tomorrow, I will send somebody to fix everything." Three days passed this way, with more disasters. Then Alex came home and announced, "I found a housekeeper and her family, and I don't know when I might find another one, so I have hired them."

I was not surprised. I deserved this. So I responded, "That's okay. We can go to my cousin's beach house."

Alex disagreed at once. "Oh no, you are now going to be my guest and live like an English lady. I have only one condition:

you cannot go near the kitchen. Mrs. Jones will do everything. She will serve you breakfast in bed." This was another magical incident in my life. Here we were, refugees with no money, yet having a lifestyle like we never had before or since. In the morning, Mrs. Jones did indeed bring us breakfast on a silver tray. She had cooked extra for Andy to help him gain weight. Paul and I went to London to visit people. When we came home, dinner was waiting for us.

This was the first time that Alex had connected with people like us, and he enjoyed having us there. He looked forward to watching Robin Hood with Andy, and he loved having a glass of whiskey with Paul. He had a horse stable and taught Andy to ride. He also encouraged Andy to go to the local school, even though he could not talk with the kids. After a few weeks, Alex stopped going to his London office. Instead, he showed us around Cambridge and then Oxford. We had a ball.

One day, his son Sandy came and said that his father had to go to an alcohol rehabilitation program. We did not know that Alex had a drinking problem. As we learned later, his wife left him when his son was a few months old, and he became depressed. Losing contact with people in the village, he turned to drinking. We had not noticed it, as he drank at night in his bedroom.

Having lived alone in this house for many years, Alex invited us to stay while he was in the rehabilitation program. He told me I would be the lady of the house now. Not long after, I invited my cousins for dinner. It was a great moment when they exclaimed in amazement, "We never saw a house like that. How do you do this?" All three had lived in England for seventeen years by then and had developed a taste for the good life. A professor at Cambridge University, Jan had spent years learning and perfecting his Cambridge English. Stephen had a huge pig farm and had received an honor from the queen for farming. His son

*My three
cousins:
Ladislaw, Jan,
and Stephen*

England 1938

went to the same school as Prince Charles. Ladislow was an elegant stockbroker in London. Now, the environment of Alex's house and the housekeeper surpassed even their expectations. Childishly smug to be one-up on my cousins at last, I replied, "I did it in my way. Just enjoy it." Although all that splendor was not mine, I played the role of lady of the mansion. My four-year-old self was proud. I know now that I still carried the shadow of their past domination of me.

During those three weeks while Alex was away at the rehabilitation center, Paul and I connected with his neighbors and eventually invited everyone to a party. The village had one of every occupation: one doctor, one pharmacist, one butcher, and so on. People came and had a good time until around 11:30 P.M., when they said they had to go. The rumor was that the ghost would be coming. We asked, "What ghost?" It turned out that they believed Alex's house was haunted. A woman had killed herself there years earlier, and now her ghost returned every midnight.

This helped explain how sad and lonely Alex had been. They knew about his alcohol problem and didn't want to associate with him. We were the first people in his world who were in his house and enjoying it. When Alex came back, we said, "We want you to have a party for the people in the village." He agreed. He became connected again, and his neighbors realized how nice a person he was.

The same villagers also took us under their wing as the area's refugees. When we left England, they gave us four big boxes of warm clothes and a fur coat. They brought us enough warm stuff to go to the North Pole.

Alex again took us to Cambridge from time to time. On some of those trips, he didn't have lunch with us. Once, when I found an umbrella in the car, he told us that he was meeting someone. We learned later that he had reconnected with the widow of an old friend who had died twenty years before. After we left England, he married her and sold his house. I visited them once, and we always hoped to invite him to visit us in Canada once we had a house. Unfortunately, he died before that. We were sad to hear this. He had provided a wonderful time in our lives when it could have been a difficult transitional winter in a strange country. Alex's hospitality fostered security, recovery, a loving environment, and a lot of fun.

We had been in England since December 1956. I still spoke very little English, though more than Andy and Paul. In April 1957, we learned that an American military airplane from the Flying Tigers was finally available to transport Hungarian refugees from England to Toronto. We had switched from wanting to go to Vancouver, as someone told us we'd have more luck finding jobs in Toronto. To help begin a new life, our relatives sent us off with seventy pounds, which was a lot of money. Alex took us to the airport.

Leaving Hungary and moving to Canada felt less like choices than the outcome of all my yearnings and the greatest gift in my journey to self. I again learned the value of taking risks, and the greatest value of all: being free. Being free and having my family was all I had, and I was fulfilled. Everything else was unimportant. Having faith in ourselves was enough to go on.

The plane crossed the Atlantic at a very slow speed. Somewhere over Iceland, the pilot announced that we were not going to Montreal or Toronto. Most of the eighty-five refugees on the flight had signed up to go to one of those cities because they had relatives there or work lined up. So a riot almost erupted on the plane. The pilot informed us that he was not allowed to land in any of Canada's eastern cities because they had no room for us. Too many Hungarian refugees were already there. So he was going to fly us to Vancouver, in the western province of British Columbia.

I thought, "Well, that's great. Vancouver is on the ocean." Aside from what we had heard about jobs, we had no investment in going to Toronto. We knew little about the city and almost nothing about Canada. In Hungary, we had thought Canada was part of the United States. I was very surprised to learn that it wasn't.

The flight took more than thirty hours. The cabin was hot, no food was served, and everybody except us was upset. When we finally arrived in Vancouver, immigration people put us all on a bus to Abbottsford, site of yet another Hungarian refugee camp. Five thousand Hungarians were already there—and angry. The Vancouver area had room for us, but no work. So there we were in a camp full of unhappy people without even the prospect of finding a cleaning job. Our four boxes of warm clothes were not very useful in Vancouver, so we gave away most of the warm socks, pullovers, and cardigans.

Again, a miracle happened. My closest friend in Budapest and Andy's godmother was Susan. She had gone to Sweden after the war and eventually ended up in Vancouver. Under the communist regime, I'd had to stop corresponding with her. Now, finding her name in the telephone book, I phoned her. Very happy to hear from us, she came to the camp immediately and took us to stay at her house.

Susan lived in North Vancouver, which was beautiful. Having a talent for doing things with money, she was very well off. "This is not a bad place," Paul and I agreed. "We can stay in Vancouver." With Susan taking us around, wining and dining us, we had a wonderful time. She also phoned the veterinary association to find out what Paul's prospects might be regarding a license and so on. Someone there said that British Columbia needed twenty-five vets, but they were interested only in people from Britain. Since Paul was Hungarian, he shouldn't even bother applying for a license. We would have to go somewhere else. "You're not very nice people," Susan said into the phone. After hanging up, she told us that British Columbia was behind the Tweed Curtain (a local term for the noticeable barrier between Anglo-Saxons and those from other countries). We were very disappointed, but we decided to go to Toronto.

Susan
1998

"Leave Andy here," she offered, "until you get settled a little." Having missed a decade of his childhood, she wanted to pamper him and get him into school. He had lost most of grade eight because he'd left Hungary in November, but somehow she got him into the same grade in a Jesuit school. Between April and June, he learned a lot of English and caught up well in his grade. When she sent him back to us in Toronto, he was dressed like a gentleman. The most important things for him were his watch, his suit, his luggage, and his graduation.

So by 1957, we were in Canada, starting a life in the freedom and security I had always dreamed about. All we had were our inner resources, but we knew that Canada would give us the opportunity to use them. I think what helped us the most was our love for each other and our faith in ourselves and in this part of the world.

I wrote to Elsa Allan, my friend from Paris. When Hungary became a communist country, we had had to stop communicating. And I could not risk bringing her address with me when I left. So I wrote to all the Allans in Los Angeles, trying to locate Elsa or someone who knew her. I did not know where she lived or what her last name might be by then. But I got no answer. After searching for her in many other ways, I was left with sadness. I could never tell her about lying to her in my attempts to fit in, or about how much I will always appreciate our friendship. She was a good friend.

In Toronto, I soon found a job with Canada Life Insurance Company on University Avenue. Even though I was an economist, I knew nothing about life insurance or what went on in such a company. Life insurance was not a known concept in Hungary, but the salary of $37.50 a week was a lot of money for us, so I took the job.

In a huge hall with eighty "girls"—all the women working there were called girls—I sat at a small desk, alphabetizing checks that arrived on my left and went out on my right. I wanted to know what we were actually doing. Where did the checks come from? What did people do on the other floors of this huge building? When I asked the other women, they told me, "This is not your business." That was the first thing I learned in Canada: nothing was my business. My business was to complete my little task, sitting in this huge room that worked like a machine under the eyes of the supervisor in his glass cubicle. His only worry was whether people came back from their coffee breaks on time and whether they worked hard enough. We got a ten-minute break in the morning, an hour for lunch, and a ten-minute break in the afternoon. It was all rules, rules, rules. Routine, routine, routine. Once in a while, I'd take a short break in the bathroom because it was the one place we were allowed to go. "If this is Canada," I thought, "I don't want to stay." After handling vital responsibilities in Hungary's Planning Secretariat, I was now putting little pieces of paper into alphabetical order from 8:30 in the morning to 4:30 in the afternoon. It was the most god-awful job in my whole life.

Paul's job in a veterinary clinic was not much better. He had to clean the dog kennels for a young vet. Paul was an excellent vet, much more able than the young man who hired him, but he couldn't treat the dogs because he wasn't licensed in Canada. At least we had jobs. Between us, we made $87.50 a week. This covered our groceries and rent.

That June, when Andy came home, we rented a house for the summer from a professor of history at the University of Toronto. Knowing we were refugees, he let us have his house very cheaply while he and his family went away on vacation.

Before they left, this professor and I had a few conversations. He liked discussing politics with me. Many students and faculty members at the university were very excited about ideas of a communist paradise. They were unaware that the Communist Party was not practicing what Marx was thinking and writing about. The ideology is impossible to achieve anyway, because human beings want to be rewarded for their individual achievements. People want to be recognized, and they need feedback; but in that system, ideally, everybody is equal—which means nobody gets rewards or individual recognition. In reality, of course, the Party people on the higher echelons are not equal. They see themselves as better than the others, and they even kill each other. So it's a terribly unjust and chaotic system.

It is against human nature to have to deal with controversies but be barred from commenting on them, such as knowing that the system lies to you and pretending that's not happening. The propaganda then was very strong, however, and the Marxist ideology is beautiful, ideally. Having once believed in it myself, I now felt an obligation to share my experiences and to tell people not to trust communism or its propaganda.*

When the professor arranged for the magazine *Chatelaine* to interview me about this, I was really excited. At last, I could do something more useful than alphabetizing checks. Not knowing anything about *Chatelaine*, I was surprised when I went for the interview and learned that I was to meet the reporter in a kitchen.

---

* I think the practice of communism was more dangerous than Nazism because the whole world knew, after awhile, what the Nazis were doing and so could do something about it. Communism was hidden. It was years later before we found out how many millions of people Stalin killed. When they opened our Hungarian jails, we saw how the Communists had tortured our friends, our people. Many died in these places, and we hadn't known about it.

As the interview started, all her questions were about housekeeping. She wanted to know what a kitchen was like in Hungary and whether we had washing machines and dishwashers. She obviously wasn't interested in communism or anything political. I had never had any interest in household things, so I thought, "Who cares whether we had dishwashers?" Then she asked what our kitchen floors were made from. My English was still not all that good, so I tried to describe floor tile. Wanting to say they were made from small stones, I couldn't think of the word *stone*. So I said, "They're made from what's out in the garden."

"Grass?" she asked in amazement.

"Yes, grass." I gave up.

"Could you give me a recipe for Hungarian goulash?" she asked next. While I knew how to cook Hungarian chicken goulash, I did not know how to convert kilograms into pounds. I'd say, "You take some onions—" and she'd ask, "One pounds, two pounds, three pounds?" She kept asking me about pounds and ounces. "Three pounds," I'd say, not wanting to let on that I didn't know. I thought she'd check everything and send it to me for corrections before printing the article, but she didn't. So *Chatelaine* came out with this horrible article about grass kitchen floors, a strange recipe for Hungarian goulash, and a picture of me by their stove.

Soon after, a group of Hungarian immigrants in Toronto invited Paul and me to a party. It would be my first social event in Toronto. When we walked into the room, everybody stopped talking. "What's wrong?" Paul asked.

"Well, that *Chatelaine* article," someone replied, "it's not very accurate. And what Maria said about Hungary is not very good for our reputation." This was an important awakening. The message I got was that probably nobody there was interested in my passion to share the truth about communism not being a paradise. I would have to find the people who wanted to hear it. To a certain degree, this experience got me to take a new direction: to look after our own lives and ourselves more than trying to change the broader environment.

That fall, we moved into our first apartment in Toronto, on Eglinton Avenue. We had no furniture, so we kept our few things on boxes. It was a "bachelor" apartment, so Paul and I slept in the one room, and Andy slept in the kitchen on a cot that was as long as the whole room. I felt very badly about that, but Andy just loved it: "It's the best spot. I can open the fridge by my head, and I can eat right in the bed." More important, we all liked living there because we could close our door and know that the police would not come to get us. We were safe.

Years later when I learned about adolescents acting out, I asked Andy, "How come we never had this problem?"

He said, "There was nobody to act out against." This was true. Starting our new life together, Andy became a friend, a partner in settling into our new home and new life.

Me in the Chateleine *kitchen 1957*

Having left a totally equipped household, we had to buy plates, silverware, glasses, or pans whenever we wanted to eat or cook something. And we loved exploring the food in Canada. For a few dollars, we could buy things we'd never had before: oranges, new vegetables, different cuts of meat, butter, and so on. Andy grew taller very fast. Once, I handed him a banana and told him to eat it. When he came back later and said he hated it, I realized I had forgotten to tell him to peel it first.

Because I hated working at the insurance company, I went to all the employment agencies and told them in my limited English that I was a trained economist and wanted another job. Six months later, a woman phoned to say that she had found an interesting job for me in a new insurance company. It had been set up with an investment of German money.

I told her, "I don't want to work in an insurance company, and I especially don't want to go to a company created with German money." I was very suspicious back then, having learned not to trust anybody. She kept calling back and, to keep the contact, I placated her by going for an interview in the actuarial department.

It was a small, plush place with stylish people and new carpets—very different from the Canada Life building and its big room with eighty women overseen by a man in a cubicle. Here, a young man introduced himself as the actuary and found out that I spoke German. This was an asset. As this was a new company, he explained, he needed to create a whole package of premiums during the next six months. My job would be to do certain calculations based on all these formulas. He showed me a calculating machine, but I'd never seen one like it. I was afraid I'd never learn how to use it.

Suspecting that all this was too nice to be a real company, I didn't believe anything this man told me. Some of it—*actuary*, *premiums*, and other terms—I didn't even understand. Worried that they were going to sell me into white slavery in Africa, I told him, "I cannot do this. I don't know how to work this machine, and I don't know anything about life insurance."

He persisted. "How much money do you make now?"

"It's $37.50 a week."

"How would you like to make $150 a week?"

My first thought was that Paul wouldn't have to work if I made that much money. We lived on $87 a week as it was. My second thought was that something here was definitely wrong. If this man was offering me $150, he was certainly planning to cut me to pieces or do something horrible. After all, with the blue carpets and everyone being so elegant, it did look rather like a dating agency. I was suspicious.

"I'll pay you well, and I will teach you," he told me. "Don't worry about the formulas. I'll hire somebody to do the formulas, and you'll do fine."

Telling him I would think about it, I left. On my way home, I was thinking that, not knowing much about this company, there was no way I was going to give up my little job for this kind of set up. Paul was much more practical, saying, "Try it for a week. In one week, you'll make four or five weeks' worth what you're making now." Still, I felt unsure.

Back at Canada Life Insurance, I told my story to the supervisor in the cubicle. He almost fell out of his chair. "I don't make that kind of money," he said. "I don't understand."

"Yes, I knew something was wrong with this," I replied. But he got so excited that, a few hours later, he sent me up to the seventh floor to see the personnel manager.

She was a wonderful lady, an older woman with lots of experience. When I told her the story, she said, "You know, I've worked here for thirty-five years, and I'll tell you one thing: if I'd had such an offer thirty-five years ago, I would have taken it. I suggest you should take it now. What's holding you back?"

"Well, I can't afford to lose this job. What if I don't like it over there, or if I can't do the work?"

"I'll give you a guarantee. If you don't like it, you can get this job back. Go over there and try it." She was the first person in Canada who helped me make a very important choice. Having my old job guaranteed gave me the courage to take on the new one. I am ever so grateful for this woman's compassion, understanding, and kindness in helping a total stranger.

I took the new job and ended up having a great time. The office was full of wonderful people, so I found new friends. The actuary, a brilliant young man, taught me about building the company from scratch. He and his family became friends and are still close to my heart. They named one of their daughters Maria. A young man from Britain also became a very good friend of ours. He taught me how to use the calculating machine, do the formulas, and do the actuarial work. Again, I was in a learning situation and enjoyed finding out everything about life insurance, including the reason my salary was so high. If my boss had hired an actuarial assistant rather than me, he would have had to pay much more.

As the company grew, I moved up through the ranks from actuarial assistant to underwriter to office manager overseeing a staff. With my good salary, Paul didn't have to work while studying for his licensing exam.

Life insurance now made some kind of sense to me, but I still did not believe in it. It seemed at odds with my experience and view of life. I resisted buying a policy. That was a big mistake, as I found out later.

After being in Toronto a little while, Paul and I decided to bring my mother over from Hungary as soon as possible. Knowing that many of the younger generation had left, the Hungarian government had ruled that people over sixty-five could leave the country within a year as long as they gave up all their homes, possessions, pensions, and so on.

I applied to the Canadian immigration department to have my mother join us. Someone there said it would take years before Paul and I were settled enough to qualify. Since my mother had to leave Hungary, my next idea was to get her to England first. She could stay with my cousins and then, since Canada was a commonwealth country, she could easily come over a week later. My cousin Stephen agreed to arrange her emigration to England.

Once she was in England, I returned to Toronto's immigration office to get a visa for her. The person I spoke with said to come back in two weeks. Two weeks later, I got the same response. Meanwhile, I kept getting letters from my mother, saying, "You brought me out to England and here I am. I've lost everything, and now I cannot go to Canada." After going to the Immigration Department every two weeks for about a year, I finally realized that, at least in those days, no one there gave answers. They just delayed the process.

The Hungarians we knew in Toronto could offer no help, either. Having arrived at the same time we did, they knew just as little about how things worked. Nor could we turn to longtime Hungarian émigrés, who took offense at our generation's high self-esteem and feeling entitled to pursue a good life.

Someone at work told me, "Go see your member of parliament." That was absolutely the scariest thing I could imagine doing. I'd just come from a country where we couldn't trust anyone in the government, especially the police. Determined to have my mother with me, however, I eventually decided to take that advice. After going to the capital, Ottawa, I stood in front of the huge parliament building with its three massive entrances. Still fearful about anything official, I went to the side door and told the doorman who I was looking for. He asked, "Do you want to go up, or do you want him to come down?"

I said I wasn't about to take another step inside this building. In my mind, I'd never get out again; I was still in the old country. The doorman said, "He'll come down." That, too, seemed very strange to me, that a member of parliament would come down to meet a stranger. I became even more suspicious—and scared.

A man came down and, since the weather was nice, suggested that we sit in the park to talk. Once I told him about wanting to bring my mother over from England, he said, "Well, immigration is very complicated. But I know the minister. I'll find out what is going on with your application."

When he told me to come back in the afternoon, I explained that I had to get back to Toronto that evening. "Where do you live in Toronto?" he asked. I gave him our address. "Oh," he frowned, "then I'm not your member of parliament." A lawyer from Toronto, he represented an area that was north of our apartment. (I had told the doorman that I lived on Avenue Road but had not said exactly where.)

"Oh no," I groaned. "I have to talk to somebody else again. I can't do it." I had begun to trust this man. He said he would look into it anyway. When I went back later, he told me that people who landed in one of the commonwealth countries— such as my mother—had to stay there two years before going to another.

I didn't know why this was such a big secret. The immigration office in Toronto could have told me that. I said my mother would die if she stayed another year in England. Personally, I also knew she would never believe me if I told her about this regulation. From the beginning, she had never trusted me to get her to Canada. I still was not very close to her.

He said, "Every year, the Minister can give exceptional visas to a hundred cases. I'll work on making your mother one of those." Still not trusting him completely, of course, I had my doubts. But for a few weeks after I got home, I received elegant letters on parliamentary paper in which he informed me about every step he took. This new experience led me to a growing sense of trust that this politician would actually support his constituents—as well as someone living just outside his area. Approachable, helpful, humane, and true to his word, he helped me take another step toward security and belief in humanity. It was another miraculous experience for me, and I learned that I could undertake things in Canada and get them done. I began to respect and become curious about this political system called democracy.

My mother arrived in Canada four weeks after my trip to Ottawa. Despite her poor health, she got in on her special visa from the Minister. Her arrival made it quite crowded in our small apartment, so it was an upheaval for all of us. Things soon turned out well, however. Having left everything behind to be with us, she worked hard to find her place in this new environment. I respected her courage. All she was allowed to bring with her were her clothes and, as I had suggested, some family photos. Those were the only things we could not buy or replace.

Not only did she take over the cooking, but she felt good about being with us. As someone who adjusted easily, she soon made friends with Hungarian-speaking women of her age. She never really learned English, but she did watch television. The two of us started a new relationship, and that's when I started finding out how generous and accepting she was with me. I felt her love for all of us.

Learning English and the Canadian way of life was an issue for all of us. For Paul and me, the number one motivation for coming to Canada had been to give Andy the best possible opportunities. Now, with both of us working during the day and all of us speaking Hungarian at home, we worried that we might be hurting his academic and social progress.

To give him a serious education, we decided to send him to St. Jerome's High School, a Catholic boarding school in the nearby town of Kitchener.

Education had always been a principle value for us, but religion had not. During the war, being Jewish had made us Nazi targets. After the war, Hungary's communist government had shut down churches, and no one talked publicly about religion. Schools provided no religious education, and we didn't talk about it at home, either.

Andy's very first visit to any place of worship had been while we were in England. Finding the Catholic church there rather small, he was much more interested in the Protestant one. Then, watching the ushers collect money after the service, he had decided it was just like the Communist Party, which did not leave a good impression on him.

When we came to Canada, Paul and I felt an obligation to make sure that what had happened to us would never happen to Andy, his kids, and their kids. We believed that the world—the entire world—was not a safe place for Jews. For me, deciding to lead this new life with a non-Jewish identity was the only way I could think of to ensure safety for my son and his future offspring. While we told Andy most of our stories about Hungary, we never talked about my Jewish background with anyone, even him. For me, this was not an issue. I never wanted to belong to any organized religion. During the war, I was so disappointed by the Catholic establishment's neutrality that I did not consider myself to be a Christian, either. I wanted to find my own spirituality, whatever fitted my beliefs.

For Paul, keeping his Jewish background a secret did not work. His personality, his sense of humor, and his lifestyle represented his culture, so he did not hide his background. Almost all our friends were Jewish, and they knew. That was okay with us.

Wanting Andy to have a good education as well as some exposure to religion so that he could make his own choices about it, we thought that St. Jerome's High School would be just the thing. St. Jerome's admitted him to grade nine, and he did learn English fluently by the end of the year. As it turned out, however, he did not adopt any religious beliefs and wanted nothing to do with religion after that. He refused to go back to that school the next year.

So I had to look for another place. Andy was fascinated with the Toronto scene on Yonge Street, which led me to worry about who he might befriend and what they might get up to if we sent him to a local public school. Instead, I wanted to lock him up in a really good place where he could be safe and learn everything he needed to know about leading the Canadian way of life.

After some research, I discovered that one of Canada's best boarding schools, Upper Canada College, was almost next door to where we lived. Going over to check it out, I found it to be a very nice Anglican school. Each boarding student's room was bigger than our apartment. At my appointment with the principal, an old Anglican minister, I explained that we had just come from Hungary and that Andy had just finished grade nine at St. Jerome's, and that I'd like Andy to be a boarder at Upper Canada College through grade thirteen. I didn't care what it cost. Our income wouldn't cover it now, but we would be able to start paying in about five years.

The principal stared at me in surprise. "This school is one hundred years old, and in those one hundred years we've never had a request like this."

"There was never a Hungarian revolution, either," I replied. "This was the first uprising against communism."

The principal asked, "How do you know that you will be able to pay later?"

"I just know it. My husband and I are both professional people. We work hard, and this is a country where, if you work, you make money. My son's education is very important to us. It is the reason why we are here and why I want my son to live here." With some deep sense of justice, I felt absolutely entitled to have Andy attend one of the best schools in Canada. If I were at home in Hungary in normal circumstances, this would be the kind of school I would want him to attend.

He said he had to take it to The Board. I didn't know what a Board was, but I thought it wasn't going to work. If he had to take it to other people, they would say no. But when he called me two weeks later, he said that The Board had decided to help out a Hungarian refugee boy. Our arrangement was that Paul and I would begin paying in five or six years, after Andy's graduation. We didn't have to put it in writing. The principal believed me.

So Andy became a boarder at Upper Canada College. Eventually, I found out that tuition and board cost around $2,000 a month—an awful lot of money in 1958. I still didn't care, though, because I couldn't have paid even $100. I just knew that we would pay for it later. Other Hungarians were outraged: how could I have been so arrogant as to want my son at such a prestigious school? They told Paul that only rich kids went there, and Andy would either never fit in or would become a snob. This worried Paul a lot. Besides, they said, children from Toronto weren't there as boarders; the school also had a program for day students. The boarders were kids from Mexico, from the United States, from all over the world—all of them rich boys.

The first time we had to go to a parents' meeting, people at work told me I had to wear a hat. I had never worn a hat in my life, and besides, I didn't have money for one. A coworker told me to go to a department store, buy a hat, and then return it the next day. I took the advice. A friend and I went shopping, where I bought a tall hat with fur on top. While getting ready, as I leaned toward the mirror to put on lipstick, the hat fell off and into the bathroom sink, which was full of water. Brushing it off, I finished getting ready and went to the meeting.

There, we learned that Andy was skating and going to parties. He was having a great time. In Hungary, schools did not consider social activities to be important. Only education was. Students had to study. So when I got to speak with the headmaster, I said we were worried about how Andy's grades would turn out if he was having so much fun. Looking right at me, the headmaster said, "For this boy at this time in his life, it is more important to have fun than for you to worry about his grades. We'll keep an eye on his academic progress, and if there are problems, we'll solve them."

I had never heard an educator talk like that. I knew then that Andy was in good hands because they were doing a very different kind of education than we knew about. They gave him a tutor in English, and he became even more fluent. Upper Canada College let him finish grade ten and eleven in one year, making up for the year he'd lost. He also found some Canadian friends. Gaining security, he began to feel a sense of belonging in Canada.

The day after the meeting, I took the hat back. Looking it over, the saleswoman said, "This hat's been wet." Turning to a

young clerk, she asked, "Was it raining yesterday?" The clerk
shook her head, no. The saleswoman told me, "We can't take it
back."

"You must!" I felt panic. I needed my $35 back. "I only wore
it last night, and my husband didn't like it." No such luck, however. The saleswoman sent it to another department and asked
me to return in a week—when they handed it back to me once
and for all. I still have the hat. I've never worn it since.

Paul decided to take his licensing exams after we'd been in
Toronto for about two years. To him, licensing was only a
formality. He assumed they would grant him a license on the
basis of his twenty-five years of veterinary practice. Unfortunately,
he was wrong: he failed the exam. This was not surprising to me,
as Paul still didn't know English much better than when we'd
arrived. What was a surprise was that he could never take the exam
in Toronto again. Apparently, each provincial association decides
how much flexibility to give people who take their licensing
exams. Paul's mistake was to say that he wanted a private practice.
Only later did we find out that the private practitioners in that
association didn't want another one. In their eyes, there were
enough already. We had never lived in a country with a free
market. This was our introduction to how such a market can be
controlled.

Paul was advised to sit for the exam in Manitoba, where
only nine vets were in practice. He did, and he passed there for
two reasons. First, he did very well. Second, he said he wanted to
work for the government rather than going into private practice.
That's how we ended up in Winnipeg.

What lies behind us and
what lies before us are tiny
matters compared to what
lies within us.

—*Ralph Waldo Emerson*

The most beautiful discovery true friends make is that
they can grow separately
without growing apart.

—*Elizabeth Foley*

— *9* —

Putting Down Roots

During our early days in Canada, we went through chaos and difficulties in learning the language, being in jobs below our abilities, and being poor. Then, after earning his Manitoba license, Paul rented a room in Winnipeg and took a government job. For almost a year, my mother and I stayed in Toronto until Andy finished grade thirteen. This was out of ignorance, as the university in Manitoba accepts students after they finish grade twelve. We didn't have that information then.

While Paul was in Winnipeg and the rest of us were in Toronto, I suddenly became very sick. It had been years since I'd had meningitis (in Budapest, in 1946 and 1951), but the symptoms of a specific kind of headache told me that it had returned. I was very weak, but I'm not sure it would have helped much to go to a hospital. Waiting for Canadian citizenship at the time, we were eligible for outpatient treatment only. Over a few hours, my condition got worse. Having no contacts, I could not get a physician to make a house call.

Desperate, my mother called Susan in Vancouver. A wonderful friend, she came to Toronto immediately. She got a doctor to come see me. He diagnosed meningitis but could not get me a hospital bed. Susan then flew me to see Dr. Ackerman, an excellent healer on the outskirts of Vienna, Austria. In addition to his job as a police physician, he spent his free time doing research with cancer patients. Many of them came from all over the world. He did not charge, because his treatment was not yet licensed. It involved strengthening the body's immune system by injecting a liquid he developed from human placenta. His idea was that the body can take care of itself once its resistance rises. Working like a vaccine, these injections triggered the body's immune reaction and the process of healing.* So, while he did his research mainly with cancer patients, the same human placenta treatment worked with all symptoms and dysfunctions. He was a genius.

Susan and I stayed in a hotel, and every day she took me to see Dr. Ackerman. It was the most bizarre scene. From all over the world, people sat for hours in the police station waiting room. We may have been staying in Vienna's most expensive hotels, but none of us were allowed to pay for the successful treatment we were getting from this brilliant man. He saved many lives.

For the first time, I underwent a truly holistic, nontraditional process of healing. It was a life-saving and eye-opening experience that built up my system step by step. Every day, I had to report my symptoms, dreams, food intake, and every little detail about my day, even symptoms of earlier illnesses that came back. The first few weeks, I was very ill and weak. After a month, my symptoms went away and I started to regain my energy. (I never had meningitis again.) Curious and fascinated, I wanted to find out more about this process.

Toward the end of my treatment period, a Mexican family with a Mongoloid son came after being referred by the Pope. At first, the busy doctor did not respond to their constant pleas in English. Finally, he asked if I would translate into German for him, as he did not speak English. He was interested in taking the

---

* Nowadays, when I work with people's emotional stuck points, I follow a similar process.

Mexican boy on as a patient, so I stayed longer in Vienna. Over time, the child improved remarkably.

In translating every step in the bo e to believe that we can heal ourselves with determination and a holistic understanding of body, mind, and spirit. I also connected with Mrs. Ackerman and their daughter and remained a friend of the family until Dr. Ackerman's death a few years ago.

In the spring of 1960, after I returned to Canada, Andy and I went to visit Paul in Winnipeg. We took along Paul's cat, who absolutely hated the rest of us. When we arrived, Paul's landlady shrieked, "No cats here! If you want to stay, you'll have to leave the cat outside." That night the cat ran into the landlady's bedroom, and she threw us out the next day because she was afraid of black cats.

Taking us around the city, Paul wanted to show us how nice Winnipeg was. Andy and I wanted to stay in Toronto, so we were totally hostile. We hated everything. We had to move to Winnipeg, of course, because Paul was there. My mother moved there first, because she adored Paul and wanted to take care of him until we got there in 1961.

Moving to Winnipeg was a big adjustment for us and, at the same time, an opportunity. Paul was finally working in his profession, although he already hated his government job as a meat inspector. He never saw a living animal. Soon, we decided he had to start a clinic. We got little encouragement. Everyone we knew said that Paul was absolutely crazy to give up his secure government job. We couldn't set up a clinic with less than $25,000 in our pockets, they warned us. We had nothing in our pockets. We barely had furniture. But we couldn't wait till we saved up that kind of money.

Early on, Andy had a great idea. Looking through the telephone book's Yellow Pages, he found only nine private veterinarian clinics in Winnipeg. Sticking little flags onto a map of the city, he saw that they were all on the west side of the Red River. Pointing to the east side, to an area called East Kildonan, he said, "This is where we should locate your clinic, Dad. And we should call it the Kildonan Animal Clinic."

We did have a car by then, so we drove around the east side of the Red River. East Kildonan turned out to be a middle-class family district where everybody had pets. Eventually, we saw a "For Rent" sign on a small storefront. The owner, an electrician, soon rented Paul the one-room space for $50 per month.

To set it up as a clinic, we bought an examining table and a few instruments. Andy made flyers with a big, beautiful dog's face over the announcement that the new Kildonan Animal Clinic would open its doors on September 1, 1962. He took the fliers around to all the nearby schools.

On the opening day, we were all nervous about whether anyone would show up. Paul didn't want us making him more nervous, so Andy and I bit our nails at home. Around noon Paul phoned, saying, "Come out and see this. All along Henderson Highway, kids are waiting in line with their cats and dogs, wanting to see the new vet."

From then on, Paul was busy day and night. He just loved it. The kids fell in love with him because he would talk to them and explain what was going on with their pets. Within a few weeks, Paul's place got so busy and full of commotion that the electrician who worked in the next room moved out. Paul rented that space as well. (Some years later, we bought the building.)

A very traditional vet, he did his surgery and everything without ever having any big, fancy X-ray machines or other equipment. He had many years of experience, and his work was extremely effective. Younger vets sometimes criticized Paul for not having a fancy clinic with expensive modern machinery, but he ignored the criticism. He did everything himself, and people loved him. As his reputation grew, pet-owners even came from the ot her side of the river. I still meet people who talk about Paul and his love for his patients.

Meanwhile, based on his school's recommendation, Andy registered in engineering at the University of Manitoba. Two days later, seeing him sitting around with a long face, I asked, "What's going on?"

After a long pause, he said, "I don't want to be an engineer, but now I've committed myself, so what I am going to do?" He sounded totally depressed.

"What do you want to do instead?"

"I'd really like to become a medical doctor."

"Well," I said, "they say this is a free country. We'll go down and register you in medicine."

At the School of Medicine, the deans' secretary looked at the obviously young Andy and asked, "Do you have a science degree?"

"No. I have a high school diploma from Toronto."

"Well, then, you'll have to go back to the University of Manitoba and enter the science program." We must have looked like bloody fools. In Hungary, people went to medical school directly after high school, so I didn't know Andy had to get an undergraduate pre-med degree first. He registered in the science program.

In early 1963, Paul and I bought a house—the first and only one we ever had. We all loved it, and we could finally have a dog. We found a German shepherd. The house was on the bank of the Red River, so we swam a lot in warm weather. People thought we are crazy, but we were used to swimming in the dirty Danube.

We also had many problems there. First, someone burgled the house. Everything was upside down and damaged. It was dev-astating to me, and it felt like rape. Then, after my mother fell down the stairs one day, her doctor discovered that she had a nonmalignant brain tumor. The surgery was successful, fortu-nately. She was very brave and recovered exceptionally well.

Shortly after that, in 1962 I looked for my first job in Winnipeg. My boss in Toronto had given me a wonderful letter, recommending me as an actuarial assistant to the Great West Life Insurance Company, which had its headquarters in Winni-peg. I probably could have gotten a job there right away, but I had always wanted to work with people.

In Hungary, I had hoped to do that in the health and welfare field, but it turned out to be all politics, planning, and govern-ment. In terms of learning, I had learned about all these systems. I'd also learned not to trust organizations or systems, which did not live up to their idealistic promises. Even when I helped build something or trusted a system or trusted people to continue valued systems, they fell apart. So I had become very cynical.

Now, when I started to think about what I wanted to do, I was figuring out my own philosophy and my own dreams. I gave up the notion that countries—or the ideas in them—change easily. I'd learned that it's the people who change, the individuals. In a communist system, of course, families and individuals are not important. The whole counts, and the individual is recognized only when being useful for the whole of the society.

I knew, however, that the strength and potential are in the individual. It is always the hundreds of individuals who eventu-ally say, "Enough of this." No matter how long it takes, history shows that it's always the people, always the individuals, who demand change—and contribute to it. Therefore, I became very motivated to learn as much as I could about people.

In Toronto, I had already spoken to a few people who did social work, and I imagined that they did what I really wanted to do: help people. Finding such a job in Winnipeg took some time, especially with my background. After looking a long time with no success, I went back to Vienna for a few weeks to help the Mexican family with their follow-up treatment. Their boy was starting to talk, which amazed me. He even looked different. His fingers and hands had relaxed, so he could move, learn and feel more alive. On my way home, I visited my relatives and my friend Steven in London.

Back in Winnipeg in 1962, I finally found a job. The woman in charge of St. Boniface Hospital's department of social work said, "Okay, you have a degree in economics. You can help us." I was excited. I knew St. Boniface was a general teaching hospital, so I imagined helping all kinds of people. Instead, as it turned out, the three of us in this social work department assessed people's applications for financial assistance. (In those days, we did not have socialized medicine). So we didn't actually do social work, our tasks weren't very interesting, and other hospital workers seemed to look down on us. Most people in the hospital did not even know where to find our department. For the next two years, being there challenged me to figure out what else social workers could do in a hospital. Feeling inspired to learn more and then return to revolutionize the role of social work in St. Boniface, I decided to get a master's degree in social work.

In 1964, I applied for a scholarship to go to the University of Manitoba. Counting my degree in economics from Hungary as the equivalent of their Bachelor of Arts program, they admitted me into graduate studies in their School of Social Work. I received a scholarship of $200 per month with the understanding that I'd return to working in the mental health field for at least two years.

At forty-four, I was the eldest in my class. Andy was just starting at the university, but he was embarrassed to drive to classes with his mother. That was okay with me, I could understand it.

With nothing to do but learn, I had an absolutely wonderful time. I also made new friends. Two of my teachers became close friends of our family for many years. The two-year program taught me about policies, about welfare, and about changing the world. I was also happy to learn a lot about Canada, and I wanted to know more.

I enjoyed being at the university, and I did want to be a social worker, to help people do something different with their lives. Although we didn't learn much about the specifics of human behavior, how to treat people, or how to help them, I didn't have a clue about where to learn the clinical skills I felt were missing from the program.

During my second year of graduate school, my field research placement was in a residential treatment center. That experience was awful for me because that place was treating aboriginal girls terribly. For punishment and to prevent them from running away, for example, the staff put them in cells in the basement. I sometimes had to interview them in those cells. That triggered my memories of the war. During the time I worked there, I had three car accidents and felt totally depressed. It was sad what they did to those kids.

This awful period was followed by a flood in 1966. Our house was along the lowest riverbank level, so it was in danger. The next great shock was when two policemen came to the door and asked permission to go through the house. They needed to look at the sandbags piled up around the back yard. Looking at each other in amazement, Paul and I could not believe what we had just heard. Police asking to help us? And asking permission to come into the house? It was the first time we'd ever had any choice when it came to the police. In Hungary, they would come into houses or offices—or take people away—whenever they chose. Now, we had just had another experience of being in a free and secure country. I was moved and grateful.

The river kept rising, and soon we had to evacuate the house. We stored our furniture and moved into a temporary place. After the flood, however, Andy wanted to live near the medical school, where he was in his second year. My mother also decided to live separately. After all the disruption from the flood, Paul and I agreed it was time to live in an apartment. We rented out the house.

After I graduated with my master's degree in social work in 1966, I fulfilled the terms of my scholarship by returning to work at St. Boniface. A week after I started my new position in the hospital's psychiatry department, the person in charge of my former department resigned and went to teach at the School of Social Work. The hospital's Director of Medicine asked whether I would consider becoming the new Director of Social Work.

I didn't want the job. I knew a lot about overall, global administration and I didn't like details. Nor did I want to run a three-person department responsible for social and financial assessments. After some thought, however, I took the position to avoid having anybody telling me what to do. I would become my own boss, in a way. And I had a new challenge, an opportunity to do something interesting.

My earlier dream of revolutionizing the hospital's use of social workers was still with me. I wanted social workers to become more integrated into treatment planning and the whole hospital system. My whole idea of how we were going to do that came

from what I'd learned in the process of building the regional Planning Secretariats in Hungary. I wanted to find a meaningful role
for social workers in every area of the hospital. Rather than simply
serving the whims of doctors, we could play a part in whatever
was happening.

No one in the hospital administration saw this as a priority,
I knew. They would want things to stay as they were. It would be
a challenge to bring my dream into being. So I went to see a
professor at the School of Social Work, a Catholic priest who
was responsible for the research projects that graduate students
had to undertake. "I'd like your next Master's project to focus on
St. Boniface Hospital. The project should be about the role of
social work in the hospital." If I could involve the University of
Manitoba School of Social Work, the hospital's administrators
would pay attention. It would be a matter of pride for them. The
professor agreed and soon moved the entire research class into
the hospital to start the project.

To find out what the role of social work could be, we
developed a questionnaire that went to every doctor, nurse, and
resident at St. Boniface. In essence, it asked what they thought
social work was and what they thought social workers did. A lot
of people didn't like me for instigating all this, but I simply told
them that it wasn't my project. The School of Social Work was
doing the research.

———•◦•◦•———

Suddenly, doctors were running down to my office to get
help with filling out the questionnaire. When the students finished their project and sent the findings to the hospital's board,
they reported that neither the doctors nor anyone else on staff
knew how to use us. Most still didn't even know where to find

our offices. That confusion, of course, was precisely what I had wanted the project to demonstrate.

St. Boniface Hospital then belonged to the Grey Nuns, who had founded it. I got my first summons to see the Sister Administrator. "My dear," she said, "people don't know what you people are doing or should be doing." She went on to say that she supported our suggestions, and that the board had agreed to give us five new positions.

Of course, I hired social work students who had worked on the project. They were very good, and by then they knew the hospital inside out. We began to plan more involvement by social workers in the hospital. I felt inspired to build something people-centered and to teach every social worker to be a team member.

My objective for the department was to earn acceptance, to become integrated, and to be recognized as a useful part of any treatment team. I knew this would not happen simply by talking. We had to prove ourselves with competence and compassion. My vision was that social workers would be advocates for the patients, protecting their rights to receive information and to make choices about their care. Otherwise, with all its specialties and diversity, the hospital system could seem very chaotic to patients.

To accomplish what I wanted, I knew that my department would need allies. The nursing staff became our first ally, step by step. We started by letting nurses know what we could do and reassuring them that we wanted to add our work to that of the team rather than replacing what they were doing.

Next, our strategy was to offer our services to the pediatrics department, which welcomed us easily. There, we worked with the families of hospitalized children. After that, we got involved in the hospital's discharge planning and palliative care. Our last target area was surgery, as we assumed that the surgeons might not accept our contributions easily.

Meanwhile, early in 1968, Paul and I got a letter from Zoltán. He and Edith were coming to New York and wanted to visit us. I could not believe this. I wondered how they would ever get a passport, let alone a visa to the United States. Next came a call from New York. Zoltán said if we could get them visitors' visas and airline tickets, they would come to Winnipeg to see us. We did, and they stayed with us from April 27 to May 7.

This was a gift from heaven. For all ten days, we talked and talked. They also wanted to buy things they did not have or could not afford at home, such as a radio, a tape recorder, and clothing. They loved seeing the markets in Winnipeg. Over food, which they also enjoyed, they explained everything that had happened since we last saw each other in 1956. It was the first time we'd heard what had happened after the invading Soviets took over Budapest's parliament building on November 5, 1956.

Along with all the Hungarian officials and families working and living there during the revolution, Zoltán and Edith were put onto a bus and taken from the parliament building to the Yugoslavian embassy. After a few days' asylum there, the Soviets forced them into buses again, saying that they would release everybody to go home. It was a trick. The buses took them to Hungary's eastern border, where they boarded airplanes. The Soviets then flew them to some unknown place. They assumed it was somewhere in the Soviet Union. As I found out much later, this was the first time in history that a whole government had been kidnapped.

For two years, these government people and their families were held prisoner. They had food and shelter but no idea of what would come next. Each family was held in isolation from the others, in rooms whose windows were blocked. From time to time, guards took away some of them, including Premier Nagy Imre. None of the other captives knew where these people were taken or what happened to them.

Meanwhile, Zoltán and Edith managed to survive two years of this detention and psychological torture. With the rest of the imprisoned people, they were shipped back by train to Budapest. On the way, guards threw them newspapers from the past two years. That's when husbands, wives, and children found out about their missing family members. After taking them from the prison, the Soviets had returned these people to Hungary and put them in a mass grave.*

After returning from this awful exile, Zoltán had no job, no rights, and no pension. But as a hero of the revolution, he was able to get by on people's donations. He and Edith were finally free to marry, and theirs was a much respected love story. Zoltán spent his time writing many books related to Hungarian historical events and heroes. One is titled *My Sixteen Years in Jail.*

Zoltán was an embarrassment for the puppet government, of course, but he was too popular to jail. When he asked for a passport, the premier approved it with the hope that Zoltán would not come back. When Zoltán applied for a U.S. visa, the first question there was: "Were you a member of the Communist Party?" In those days, that was the policy.

---

* Today, books and films document these events in Hungary. A special cemetery commemorates that mass grave, called "The 300." It included not only government people but also our best writers and philosophers. Walking through this cemetery recently with some Canadian friends, I felt a heartbreaking pain and sadness for those wonderful people who died for their beliefs and courage. The process is still going on to identify the individuals there and to give them very simple burials in identical individual graves. Each body was found with a knee broken. A Russian superstition says that breaking a corpse's leg keeps the spirit from coming back.

Zoltán responded, "I was one of the founders of the Hungarian Communist Party. I'd like to be invited to your country. I have traveled in the Soviet Union and in China, and now my wife and I would like to see the United States. Before you make any routine decision, please find out whether I can expect an invitation from Washington."

He did get the invitation. The U.S. government provided a Hungarian escort and took them around the country by bus. Wherever else they wanted to go, Zoltán asked friends to send them airline tickets, just as we had.

After our wonderful ten days together, they left with all the goodies we could buy them. In the coming years, we saw them again from time to time. Zoltán always remained an absolute idealist, and we were close until his death. To this day, Edith is still one of my dearest friends in Hungary.

While in the United States, Zoltán was invited to stay and to publish the book he was then writing about the Party and the revolution. Edith wanted to stay, but he said he was going back to Hungary for three reasons. First, he did not want to do the puppet government in Hungary a favor by being a public dissident. Second, he explained, he might have money in the United States but be a nobody; he was poor in Hungary but was important as a reminder of oppression and lack of freedom. Third, he wanted the book published in Hungary, where "the dirty laundry will stay within the family." His three-volume history of the Hungarian Communist Party and the Hungarian revolution, *Facts and Witnesses*, was finally published in 1991, after his death that year. It includes the story of my visiting him when Edith was jailed and tortured.

Zoltán never lost his financial talents. At the end of their visit to Winnipeg, he gave me $800, saying that I was the only one he could trust to invest it and keep it for them. That way, they would have some money when they came to the West again. Knowing that they could not bring money out of Hungary and that friends had taken care of all their expenses, I asked, "How come you have this money?"

"Do you think you were the only one to pay my airfare to Canada?" Zoltán replied. Years later, when they needed the money, he was surprised at how little interest it had earned. He said he would have turned it into a million dollars by then.

Zoltán and Edith's visit to our Canadian home reaffirmed our choice to leave Hungary. I knew well what I had left behind, but little did I suspect what was just around the corner.

Edith
1988

You gain strength, courage
and confidence by each
experience in which you
really stop to look fear in
the face. You are able to .say
to yourself: "I have lived
through this horror, I can
take the next thing that
comes along."

—*Eleanor Roosevelt*

— *10* —

Dancing with Death

Andy's last day of medical school was on May 8, 1968, the day after Zoltán and Edith left Winnipeg. Traditionally, the whole graduating class then had a big party out at the lake. We didn't want Andy to be on the highway in his little Volkswagen, so he took our bigger car while Paul and I drove to a dinner engagement in his vw. The last thing I remember about driving home that night was that it was raining, we were at a stop sign, and two headlights were coming right toward us.

They belonged to a big truck. It smashed into us head on. The Volkswagen crumpled as though it were a cardboard box. The whole windshield shattered, propelling glass into my face. My neck was broken at the top of the vertebral column. My knees were broken. My ribs were broken. My jaw was broken. I passed out without knowing any of this, of course.

Trying to find my pulse, Paul thought I was dead. My survival was, again, miraculous. Even if I hadn't died on impact, I could easily have died or been paralyzed when police officers lifted me out of the car with my broken neck. The slightest wrong movement could have cut through my spinal cord.

When I came to, I thought I was dreaming. I felt as if the inside of my head was bleeding and running into my throat. Instead, my jaw was broken and I was suffocating. The first thing that came to my mind was that I was determined to go to Andy's graduation, which was a week later. Opening my eyes, I found myself in an emergency room. Out of all the eyes looking back at me, one pair belonged to a doctor friend of Andy's. That meant this must be the General Hospital.

All the medical people looked at me and talked about me as if I were a vegetable who didn't know what was happening. I may have looked like that, as I was covered in blood, but I was listening to everything. However, nobody ever made any effort to find out whether I could hear or make a sign in response.

Totally helpless and finding it hard to breathe, I had a terrible headache. Where had it come from, I wondered. For a while, I hoped this was a dream. Then reality struck—again and again. It took me awhile to realize that I'd been in an accident and that now I was here and totally helpless. What about Paul? Nobody bothered to tell me where he was or whether he was alive. I felt frantic.

The doctors' first priority was to make it possible for me to breathe. Without a word to me, one of the doctors cut into my throat. I went into agony. Then it felt as though his hand was in my lungs. Because no one knew what else might be happening with me—whether I had a concussion, for example—they couldn't give me any painkillers or put me out. The tracheotomy tube the doctor inserted next just seemed to make breathing even harder. After that, I ended up with thirty-five stitches in my face. Nobody could really clean it well for weeks.

My mother appeared at some point. For the first and only time in her life, she had taken a taxi (which she talked about for the rest of her life). She came into the hospital very confused and, with her limited English, spent some time trying to find us. When she came to my bed and I looked up, her expression let me know how bad things must be. But at least she knew enough to reassure me that Paul had survived with a broken hip. He was in a bed on the other side of the emergency room.

My mother somehow got someone on staff to understand that Andy was at a party at the lake with his graduating class. The Royal Canadian Mounted Police found him at 6 A.M. He came to the hospital at once.

Meanwhile, I knew what was going on around me, but I didn't look like somebody who was taking in information. I had a broken jaw and couldn't even attempt to talk. Once they did the tracheotomy, I couldn't even make any sounds.

After Andy arrived, he arranged for me to be treated by the hospital's head of neurosurgery, who had a very good reputation. For conditions like mine, he was one of the most skillful surgeons in practice. He's the reason I can walk today. However, he was also said to be difficult to cope with.

When this surgeon arrived at 7 A.M., he told the other doctors, "We're going to put her into traction but, since we don't know what else is wrong, we can't give her anything for the pain." They didn't dare move me, so a technician brought the X-ray machine up to the emergency room. After they developed the film, I overheard that I had broken a second vertebra. "That might have paralyzed her," one doctor said. All the nerves go through that part of the spine. Someone else said, "Maybe she'll be in a wheelchair for the rest of her life." I was devastated. Hearing that so suddenly, without any preparation, was horrendous. I hoped I would die.

A team of people took me from the emergency room into surgery. When someone started tying my hands and legs to whatever I was lying on, I couldn't believe what was happening. The surgeon shaved off my hair. During all this, the resident doctors stood around, watching. "They've seen my X-rays," I thought. "They can put me out while the doctor operates, can't they?" Nobody stepped forward with anesthesia.

The surgeon told the residents that he was going to put in a traction device. He took out something that looked like a screwdriver and made two holes in my skull. The pain was unbelievable. I begged for unconsciousness, but nobody cared. I wanted to scream, but I had no voice. So I just endured. I think this is how tortured people feel.

Then he explained that I was to lie on a special bed with three mattresses. I was on my back, my head stretched backward. They held it there with a twenty-five-pound weight attached to the holes in my skull. All I could see was the ceiling. I couldn't move, and everything was hurting terribly. I hoped this awful traction would be for three or four hours at the most, because no one could possibly lie like that for longer. Eventually, someone wheeled me to the recovery room. The weight still pulled my head over the end of the bed, and I still couldn't move. In the end, I would lie like this for three and a half months without anyone ever telling me it would take that long.

Meanwhile, every time a nurse cleaned my tracheotomy tube, the pain was intense. Both my legs were in casts, and my ribs had been taped. Since many of my bodily functions had stopped, I was fed through an intravenous tube and had a catheter. I couldn't talk, move, or even turn my head to look around.

Later, when I got to see Andy, he had to walk to the end of the special bed to see my face. As we looked into each other's eyes, he told me the doctors still had to operate on Paul's broken hip. "You know, he thinks that you're dead," he added. Many people do die from my kind of injuries. Those who survive often remain paralyzed. Paul may have thought Andy and my mother were lying to keep him calm. "Can you write something for him?"

I couldn't, so he guided my hand to write so that Paul would know I was alive.

After observing me in the recovery room for three or four days, they took me to the neurological ward. I wanted to go to the private ward up on the sixth floor, where Paul had his own room. However, all my doctor's patients stayed on his ward, which had no private rooms. Every morning at 7 o'clock, the doctor came by to adjust my traction. He always left without saying anything. I still couldn't talk, but I was full of questions—and fears. How long would I be there? When could I have visitors? What if I could never walk again? What if I get worse and become totally paralyzed? I was also afraid of going crazy from looking at the ceiling tiles with their little holes. I had no books, no sound, no stimulation.

I never got answers to my questions. Only later did I find out from Andy that my doctor was trying to give my own system a chance to form new bone tissue. Other doctors usually sped up the process with all kinds of surgeries, but this one waited for the vertebra to heal itself. I was too old for bone formation, apparently, but I did form fibrous tissue instead. Compared to surgical interventions or implants, this healing process was a more natural one, which is why it took over three months.

Apart from that daily 7 o'clock adjustment, day and night were the same to me. I experienced many losses: not being able to talk, to swallow, to move, to walk, or even to breathe without the tracheotomy tube. Unable to do much of anything, I was totally dependent on others.

Not many others were there, however. For six weeks, no one could visit. Andy often sneaked in at night, which was good for my spirits. Somehow, I put my hands together enough to write to Paul—very slowly. It took the whole night to write a few lines.

I hated not knowing what was happening and being on my own in this whole business. They treated me absolutely like a number. What kept me alive, from then on, was my anger. I invented all kinds of revenge. If I couldn't move or speak, at least I could keep my imagination busy with my "I'll show you" plans. I never carried out any of these fantasies later, but the process kept me alive then. I really learned how anger can be helpful and energizing.

One of my rebellious gestures involved Canadian politics. By the time I could have visitors, it was national election time. The Liberal Party candidate for prime minister was Pierre Elliott Trudeau. While I admired him for his brilliance, values, integrity, and vision, I also knew that my doctor was dedicated to the Conservative Party. I asked friends to bring in campaign gadgets and to hang posters of Trudeau all over my walls. Even though he saw these, my doctor never commented.

Most of the time, however, I just looked at the ceiling and counted the little holes. I really wanted to die. Thinking about my life, I knew that it was okay for me to go. Paul was going to recover, and Andy had finished medical school. I was ready to die. But I had no way to do so. I felt trapped into going through with recovery—alone and under very inhumane circumstances.

It was a turning point in my journey. Until then, living my busy life had involved always "doing." Now, being motionless, helpless, inactive, totally dependent, and separated from everything and everybody forced me to experience sheer "being." It was a hard reality. I had nothing else but to turn inward. Struggling to stay sane, I spent time just thinking, feeling, and learning to accept what is. I took an inventory of who I was and who I wanted to be. As Morrie Schwartz wrote, "If you are ill, you can experience more freedom to be who you really are and want to be, because you now have nothing to lose."*

I had already lost everything. All I had left was my love for Andy and Paul. Living in this kind of awareness, I had nothing to choose but survival. I saw my priorities clearly: my family and, if possible, using my experiences as a tool for helping others. So I decided I would make it. Not being on any medication, I also learned to deal with pain, physical and emotional. This was a great learning. Ever since, I have refused pain medication. I can deal with pain if I want to.

The greatest emotional pain was not going to Andy's medical school graduation ceremony.* For years, I had looked forward to that. As Andy used to say, it was a day for the parents. When he came afterward in his gown and showed me his degree, I cried over his having to be there alone. And he had cancelled the next day's trip to Europe, which Paul and I had offered him. My heart broke.

After six weeks, they took the tracheotomy tube out. A nurse had to help me learn how to swallow again, using a small syringe to put little drops of water into my mouth. It helped to be able to breathe freely and to talk, but that was about all that changed. I still couldn't reach out or hold a book, and the room had no television because the bed next to mine always had someone who'd just come from brain surgery. During my months there, I watched many people die from brain tumors or other brain problems.

Still immobile and staring at the ceiling, I learned to know people through how they touched me. I learned a lot about

---

* I truly resonate with this statement, which I found years later in *Morrie: In His Own Words*, p. 93.

**Later, I sent a picture of Andy's graduation from medical school to the pediatrician in Budapest who had saved Andy's life as an infant.

communicating without words. Only one nurse's aide had any sense of empathy. She would sit with me at night sometimes. Other than that, the nurses were generally awful. The most terrible one would take off my sheet, sponge some water on me, and then just leave. Lying there naked, I thought at first that maybe she'd gone to get a piece of soap or something. But it would be half an hour before she returned, saying, "Sorry, I was on my coffee break." She seemed completely unaware of my feelings. I felt helpless and humiliated.

Once my tracheotomy tube was out, I told her exactly how I felt. The story I got back was that when doctors treated nurses horribly, the nurses treated their patients the same way. It didn't make much sense to me. Later, when a psychiatrist friend from St. Boniface sneaked in to visit, I asked, "Explain this to me. I want to understand."

"Look," he said, "on this ward, most of the patients die or remain disabled. The doctors and nurses here have to stay totally detached from these people." This theory does not hold, I thought, because a good number of us will survive. I would much rather have been in St. Boniface Hospital.

After three and a half months, a resident told me in secret— he said he wasn't supposed to tell me anything—that the last X-ray had shown some bone formation. The next morning, as usual, the doctor came in at 7 o'clock. He fiddled with something and I heard a sound. "I took your traction off," he said. "The rest is up to the nurses." It was the last time I saw him.

Would I be able to walk? Would I need more surgery or anything? Not knowing, I lay still after he left. The questions and fears filled my head. Soon, two nurses came in and rearranged me. That was a big day: I could finally lie normally in a bed. But I felt dizzy. Then an orthopedic specialist came to take the casts off my legs. The big moment had arrived. They sat me up, but I couldn't manage that, either. My body had forgotten how to sit. Over the next year, I had to learn to keep my head on my neck. Otherwise, it just went over backward.

All the nurses on the ward came to watch. Once I got used to sitting, they said, "Stand up," and I did. Of course, it felt as difficult as walking up a very steep cliff. But I could walk. I put one hand on the wall and used the other to hold my head.

I had lost twenty-five pounds, and my body had deteriorated badly. Until that day, no one had ever shown me a mirror. I still had some stitches in my face and dried blood around them, and I had no hair. After that, I just hated to look at myself—which was a sign that I was coming back to life. My wish was for the day when I could wash my hair, after it grew back.

"I'm not staying here," I told the nurses. "This is a horrible place. This is hell. I'm going home."

"You can't possibly manage," they all said.

"I'm going home," I insisted. Fortunately, my mother would be able to take care of me. Paul, who was still on crutches after his hip surgery, also wanted to go home. I told the nurses, "I don't want to stay one more moment. I don't ever want to see this ward again."

So a resident called my doctor, who simply said, "If she wants to go home, she can go home."

Paul came down to my room, on crutches. It was the first time we had met in more than three months. We were both overwhelmed to see each other again. I remember how crazy and anxious we were. We told each other of our ordeals, almost competing about who had suffered more. Andy had been our only link. No doctor or other medical person had ever visited Paul to inform him about my condition. So, after all that time in the hospital, both of us were feeling uncertain about the future.

We shared our anger over why this had happened to us. Why us? This question had occupied me all that time.

Andy took both Paul and me home, driving very slowly, but my head felt like falling down anyway. In a panic, I would tell Andy not to speed. Whenever he had to accelerate, my head flipped back.

When we got home, we had a hard time coping, with Paul on crutches and my being a total mess. When something fell down, neither of us could pick it up. My mother had her apartment in the same building, and she was a tremendous help.

After getting out of traction, I had noticed for the first time that I couldn't use my right arm. My right arm and hand were not functioning at all. Also, my bladder and some of my other

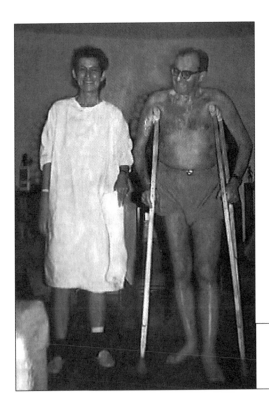

At home with Paul
after the hospital
1968

organs were not working well. After being on a catheter so long, my bowels didn't work and I couldn't pee. And I was seeing double. Still, I knew it was a miracle to get out of all this with legs to walk on, with my head on my neck, and with my sanity.

I went to see various doctors at St. Boniface. At first, no one wanted to see me, since my surgeon had not officially discharged me. I phoned his office in vain to ask for this formality. One day, when he saw Andy in the hospital's cafeteria, he said: "Tell your mother she is discharged." He told Andy my problem with my arm had nothing to do with my neck. He did not suggest wearing a collar around my neck or any further treatment.

Doctors I saw at St. Boniface considered my recovery a miracle and suggested I should be happy to be alive. I was. They

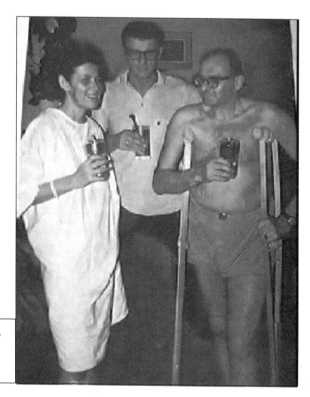

Celebrating our homecoming with Andy

also recommended an operation for my bladder, and physiotherapy for my arm. After my ordeal in the hospital, however, I didn't trust anybody to do further surgery. I did trust Dr. Ackerman in Vienna, who was against surgeries in general, and I wanted to consult with him. Paul agreed: "You have to go to Vienna. You know, you are totally deteriorated, and the only man who can help you is this one." He put me on a plane, sitting in a wheelchair.

Outside Vienna, friends helped me find a hotel near the doctor's office. For three weeks, I went to the police station to see him every day. During my first visit, he took my pulse on both wrists and both ankles, and then said, "You're blocked somewhere. Your bloodstream is blocked. Your whole body is blocked. What's going on?"

I told him I'd come to see him because of my bladder and my right arm. He put my right arm in a cast for three weeks and told me not to move it because I had a thrombosis there. This was new information. I could have died from the physiotherapy recommended by one doctor I'd seen in Winnipeg who told me that my arm had traction deficiency, I should be happy to be alive, and that I'd learn to live with not being able to move it.

Me with
Dr. Ackerman
1992

Dr. Ackerman treated the rest of my problems as well. No matter where the symptom was, the human placenta gradually strengthened my immune system. After that, my body took care of everything itself. Three weeks later, I returned to Winnipeg, feeling healthy and able to move my arm again. Everything functioned, though I still had to hold on to a wall when I walked. That had to heal very slowly.

After my three and a half months as a patient in Winnipeg's General Hospital, I had even more ideas about how to improve patient care at St. Boniface. My experience was instrumental in learning about patients' needs and care. After I went back to work at St. Boniface, I regularly visited patients on the orthopedic ward who had broken necks or were recuperating from similar conditions. My aim was to give them hope by saying, "Look at me" and telling them about my experiences and recovery.

Knowing what I had not received at General Hospital helped me to know—or know how to ask—what patients needed. I had learned how lonely, helpless, and frightened patients can be, even under the best medical care. They are totally dependent on others, deprived of making their own choices and decisions. Exposed to many various professionals, patients often don't know what to expect. The process is dehumanizing.

It was my passion to share my ideas with people in my department and especially with the nursing staff. My hope was to affect patient care through them. In the jungle of often controversial medical information and treatment, I saw social workers as being advocates of the patient. I also developed a close working relationship with the nurses on all levels at St. Boniface. They are the first-line caretakers.

I think my meetings with the staff had an impact. They believed me, especially as I spoke from personal experience. I had learned a deep respect for suffering from physical pain. Among the other things I did as soon as I got back was to teach nurses from the patient's' point of view. One of my themes was about what they could do with simple contact, communication, and a gentle touch or rub on someone's arm.

I had also discovered the spiritual strength we human beings have for survival. And I was committed to helping people to find their strength as well as their own healing energy. I had learned to be alone, and I was reassured in my faith.

A few years later, I met a magical person who influenced me profoundly. This was Jack Schwartz, founder and president of the Aletheia Psycho-Physical Foundation. A healer and teacher, he is an expert in nontraditional methods of health and healing. He has his own magic. He opens doors on the path of evolution and consciousness. After studying human energy fields, he now teaches how to activate the *chakras*, the seven energy centers along the spine, each of which has a special and specific function. He has also been both a researcher and a research subject in the voluntary control of internal states.

In the 1970s, he was teaching workshops in many places. He also did personal readings. In 1976, a friend who was organizing his Spokane workshop booked a personal appointment with him for me. At 7 o'clock one morning, I went to his hotel, where he did readings. There, I met a friendly European gentleman with a Dutch accent and a great sense of humor. We had one hour for the reading, which was a most memorable experience. The first half-hour, he described who I was. I was amazed. He did not know anything about me; I had gotten this appointment at the last minute. But he talked about my deepest inner feelings, my ways of coping, my conflicts, my craziness, and my dreams. All of this came to life in a most accurate, simple, and funny description. At one point, he ran to one corner of the room, then to the opposite corner, back and forth. "This is Maria," he explained. "When she is here, she wants to be there, and vice versa."

"Yes," I laughed. "This is my problem. What can I do to change this?"

"Nothing, honey," he replied. "This is who you are. You'd better accept it. It's the fourth ray [of energy]—the tawny, mainly orange one—that you have. Only spots of the green would add more structure and practicality to your intuition." This was all new to me, yet it made sense.

When I said that I wanted more structure in my life and that I had difficulty being organized, he told me to accept my basic structure and energy, and to use them to the best of my abilities. He encouraged me to trust the qualities that come with this energy: intuition, stability, harmony, rhythm, beauty, and balance.

The next half-hour, he read my chakras and described every health problem I'd ever had. At one point, he said: "What happened to you in 1968?"

I did not remember. When he insisted, I realized: "Oh, yes, this was the year of the accident. I had a broken neck, I was medically dead, they said."

Jack nodded: "That fits, because that was when you paid off your mortgage. Yes, you could have died. Actually, you did. You paid off your mortgage, honey. Now you're free to do anything you like." As time passed, I understood more and more how true this was. My life really changed after the accident, and I was free to learn and to become more who I wanted to be. I know now that it was not an accident that I met all my other special teachers soon after 1968, taking my life and my work in a new direction.

When the student is ready,
the teacher will appear.

—*Author unknown*

— *11* —

Awakenings

In 1968, before my accident, the head of the psychiatry department at St. Boniface had brought me a book he wanted me to read. It was *Conjoint Family Therapy* by Virginia Satir. With great enthusiasm, he said, "I was in Minneapolis and I saw this woman. She's fantastic, even though she's only a social worker."

I thought, "Thank you, but I don't like the implication there." I agreed to read the book. When I did, I knew instinctively that this was the missing piece I had been looking for since graduate school. I did not fully understand everything she wrote, but I somehow felt it, and it made sense. She talked about working with people together in counseling—couples, families, and extended families—rather than having only one-on-one sessions. In those days, it was a revolutionary idea to treat people in the context of their families, relationships, and communities. And I knew from my own experience how powerful the impact of families and communities can be.

Satir's ideas on communication and interventions also made sense to me. She talked about the therapist becoming a person first and then building a relationship with each client based on safety, respect, and compassion. This humane and personal perspective was different from stuff I'd learned in school, such as giving advice or deciding what was good for other people. Satir's underlying beliefs resonated with me. Excited, I was curious to know more about this revolutionary approach.

Early in 1969, I gave the book to a friend of mine who was going to Minneapolis. She soon phoned me to say that she'd met Virginia, who was going to conduct another workshop there later that year. I told Paul that I wanted to go very badly. He was outraged: "You can't go away at Easter. We are a family. We are going to be together at Easter." So I stayed home. (It was the last time I listened to Paul regarding something like that.)

When I ran into this friend a couple of months later, she seemed totally changed. "What happened to you?" I asked.

"I went to a three-day workshop with Virginia Satir, and I am a different person," she answered. It was true. She had rarely shared her experiences or talked about her feelings—she had never been like this before. I had always thought of her as someone who didn't like herself much. I promised myself that if I ever again got the chance, I would go see this Satir woman.

In June 1969, I heard that a group was bringing her to Brandon for a five-day workshop. I went. That was the first time I met Virginia. A very tall woman, she was loving, caring, firm, competent, and magical. I experienced her as authentic and human. She was connected to us all, she was approachable, and she was real. Around her, there was no pretending or hiding. Honesty was the only way. In her presence, I felt important and empowered. I had never met anyone like her.

The workshop was magical. I saw participants changing like I had never seen before. I hadn't known that people could have such deep processes of transformation. Like most social workers then, I had learned to focus on changing behavior through advising people. Virginia helped us to help ourselves by accepting ourselves and embracing self-responsibility. She provided opportunities for us to see ourselves clearly and to make new choices rather than telling us what was good for us. Magical things happened to people, and I was speechless. I had never learned or experienced anything like it.

Her method of using role-plays to sculpt family dynamics was a revolutionary concept for me. During these reenactments, we experienced weddings and funerals, love and hate, joy and grief—the entire range of human feelings and coping styles. She also used role-plays to highlight people's inner resources. An innovator and educator, she had developed a model based on the belief that people have resources that can be harnessed for making life more functional, healthier, and more successful.

What connected me to her strongly in those five days were her beliefs. I'd always hoped to find people who knew how to respect each other's inherent dignity, who said what they wanted to say, who lived the way they talked about living, and who did what they taught. That's what I'd met in Virginia. I was hooked, and I met others who shared my excitement. One of them was John Banmen; it was his first Satir workshop, too.

Later, after the workshop, I told Virginia, "Only you can do this. This is your magic."

"No," she replied, "Everybody has magic. I want people to find their own."

Much later, I knew this was true, and I did find mine. Meanwhile, with no idea how she did her magic or how she could teach others to do it, I was determined to learn. I asked, "Where do you teach it?"

"Once a year, I conduct a training workshop for a month. You can come to that." She gave me the name of the contact person for the September training near Minneapolis.

Meanwhile, in my very first conversation with her, I had said, "My son is going to do his residency in New York, and I'm really worried." After his one-year residency in internal medicine, Andy was preparing for his residency in neurology at the Albert Einstein College of Medicine in New York. I really wanted him to get out of Winnipeg, and I encouraged him to apply to medical schools outside of Canada. At the same time, I also worried about how he would manage all by himself.

"You are giving him a double message," Virginia told me. "You're telling him to go and to stay. Don't do that, because that's not good for him."

When I got home, I said to Andy, "I've learned something. You just go to New York. You don't have to phone me every week, and I'm not going to worry about your laundry."

"If this is what you learn in workshops," he smiled, "I'm all for it." Then he told me that he hadn't really felt free to go because he had sensed my worry. He thought I did not trust him. So learning this lesson was important for me. I realized how I

Virginia Satir
ca. *1969*

had been doing the same thing my father had done to me: using a subtle kind of control. I had learned it subconsciously. Now, becoming aware, I worked on stopping this by respecting and trusting his choices and abilities.

I became obsessed with the idea of finding out more about Virginia's process of helping people. Her insights were profoundly helpful to me. At the workshop, for instance, I had said to her, "Everybody was crying, and I cried a lot too. How come you didn't cry?"

"First of all," she answered, "I have cried. But I will never be able to help people if I cry along with them. You need to learn that. That's the difference between empathy and sympathy."

She quickly became my model, and I wanted to have her as my mentor. This new purpose let me understand why I had stayed alive so many times, most recently in the car accident. What attracted me the most to Virginia was her humanness. She was a teacher who was a person, who shared herself. She was a therapist who believed in people's strength and potential.

Her model included using people's past learnings to illuminate the present, rather than contaminate it. "It's so easy to carry on the hurts of the past and walk through life as victims," she said, "rather than making new choices and letting go of our interpretation of our past learnings, what's no longer useful in the present. We can let go and learn new ways of coping." This certainly fit my own experience of using my history as a learning experience. I already knew I could write two books about the same events in my life, one titled "Poor Me"—the victim—and the other, "What I Learned and How I Am Using It Now To Understand Myself and Others in the World.")

Virginia talked a lot about transformations, and it helped me see my life in a new light. It turns out that my big transformations came when I let go of things that seemed important in my life. At the time, I did not know these were transformations. When I look back, I see how letting go changed my life entirely. One example was letting go of my life in France and really starting to live again back in Hungary. Probably the biggest transformation was leaving the country in 1956. I had to transform all my ways of living, my expectations, my language, my life style, my dreams, and my needs. I started over again, many times. Most recently, the long, painful, and isolated hospital experience had been an opportunity for a deep spiritual transformation and for clarifying my priorities.

So everything I heard from Virginia in Brandon made sense to me, and it helped me understand myself. I wanted more. When I phoned the workshop coordinator, she said the September training was full. I phoned every day to find out if anyone had dropped out. Nobody and nothing was going to stop me from going. Finally, she let me in just to get me off her back.

Paul wasn't keen on my leaving for a month to go to a workshop. "If you go to Minneapolis," he challenged, "I'll go to Europe." He knew that, normally, I'd give up anything to go to Europe. "I'll go meet up with our friends in Florence."

"Fine," I replied. Not even Paul was going to keep me from the training workshop. But I was acting braver than I felt. Still not yet fully recovered from the accident, I had a terrifying fear of riding in vehicles—and I knew I would have to take a bus from Minneapolis to the workshop site. I went anyway.

Everybody at the training stayed at a Y camp, where we had a bed each with curtains dividing the rooms. It was uncomfortable, but I had struggled to get there and wasn't about to leave. Virginia was amazing, and I wanted to learn everything I could. In the process, I met wonderful people and again experienced Virginia's magic. I also learned a lot about myself.

The workshop started with Virginia asking what people wanted to change for themselves. I said I wanted to get rid of my fear of driving or sitting in a car. Virginia said, to my disappointment, "I cannot help you with this. You will need to accept the fear and, yes, it can happen again." Seeing the disappointment on my face, she added, "Well if you don't want to, it's going to be stronger. If you want to increase your fear, just have a fight with your fear." It was another part of learning to accept what is.

During that month-long training, I also did my Family Reconstruction. This process of discovery is about reenacting a person's (the "star's") perceptions of and interpretations about his or her family, going back three generations or more. The star becomes aware of and accepting of what he or she learned while growing up. Since our childhood family or group was our first faculty of learning, it's helpful to revisit that old context of learning with grownup eyes. We can make new interpretations: to appreciate the joys, struggles, strengths, vulnerabilities, hurts and pains of others and self, and all the other learnings that contributed to who we are. We find out how past events and experiences still affect us in the present.

During my reconstruction, I needed to recall and release my yearnings, expectations, and feelings from the past. All this led to discovering who I really was and who I wanted to become. Knowing how my patterns and resources developed helped me make new choices. In a nutshell, this is the process of transformation.

For example, when I described my father to a new friend I had chosen to play that role, he said, "Maria, I cannot play that role. You are describing a saint, and I'm a human being." This got me to realize that I did not see my father as a person but as more than human.

Through the reconstruction, I realized that the way he got me back to Hungary from France had been controlling. Control was one of the ways he had expressed love and protectiveness, yet I had always responded only to his love. Now, I realized that I, too, had mastered this indirect, subtle way of controlling people. It made up much of my pattern with Andy. I had been controlling my son in the same way my father had controlled me. I also discovered that my intense yearning for freedom and security had started at age four, with my cousins' abuse, and that my curiosity for knowing more started with my competitive desire to catch up with whatever they were reading. My own search for learning grew out of this.

Until then, these thoughts and ideas had been evolving on a subconscious level. With my new awareness, however, I could find out who I was and what I had to offer. I could share myself rather than control other people. I learned to become aware of what learnings or habits were no longer useful and to uncover whatever else had been hidden within me. It was a revelation.

Watching people reconstructing scenes from my life and the earlier lives of my parents, I was connecting with my father on a person-to-person level, an adult level. This made all the difference in how I saw him. Or, as Virginia put it, "To become a mature person and our own decision-makers, we need to connect and accept our parents as people and not as stereotypes in their roles as mom and dad."

As a result, the picture of my childhood family changed for me. As mentioned, I was always in the middle between my father and mother. I thought she was awful and blaming toward him, and that she didn't love him enough. Now I realized that, while I was protecting my father, my mother did not have a chance to get as close to my father or me as she probably wanted.

Later, I asked her how she felt about my relationship with my father. Very genuinely, she told me that she had always been very happy about it. "I was close to my family," she explained, "so I didn't interfere. I was very happy that you were close to him. I was not the kind of person who could give you the kind of love that he gave you." I felt ashamed because I had been blaming her.

Family Reconstruction left me with many complex self-discoveries. All the subtle family dynamics that came to the surface gave me the opportunity to make changes. I learned about the impact of the families of origin and the many aspects that make up the self. As Virginia wrote:

> From the moment we are born, we partici-
> pate in a hierarchical structure to survive:
> society as well as family . . . while our spirit
> wants to grow organically.

Growing up, we have millions of experiences, or learnings. With each experience, we develop an interpretation. Many interpretations serve to protect us so that we survive. Others are distorted because we don't see the total picture. In my case, I had the idea that "everything good that happens to me comes from my father."

Years later, my mother told me, "You have no idea how many fights I had with your father for you. You know, he would have never let you to go to France if I didn't fight with him for it." So, in the background, she had been helping me. "You thought I didn't want your education," she went on. "I paid for all of it, but your father had to give permission first." She never took credit for it, and I always assumed it was all from my father.

Sometimes, patterns or rules become rigid and automatic. This can lead to other problems. For instance, as Virginia wrote, "Often the price we pay is expressed in physical and emotional symptoms. . . . Symptoms are signals that something is out of harmony, the energy is not in balance. Our physical self takes on these symptoms in many forms." To make new choices, we first need to be aware of what's going on. Where did our learnings coming from? How did our often-automatic patterns develop?

I found out that our families of origin can keep us prisoners, just as political systems can. I learned a new way to understand these years as a child and to see my own prison—to which, as an adult, I alone own the key that can open the door.

Virginia taught that the way to freedom and peace is, first of all, to find our own self-worth. "Freedom within, freedom between, and freedom among" people is what creates peace in the family. She also taught that

> the family is a microcosm of the world. In the effort to change behavior, it is easy to crush the spirit, thus crippling the body and dulling the mind. This is largely due to equating the value of the person with the nature of his/her behavior.*

All this fit with my recurring theme: my search for freedom and for a humane environment in which people were seen and treated as equal and as having dignity. During my adolescence, the rise of Nazism had increased the insecurity around and inside the people I knew. By age sixteen, I had had one dream: to live in a free country, where people feel secure and respect each other and themselves.

Virginia was not only teaching these values but practicing them as well. My most important learning from her was what she wrote in her poem "The Five Freedoms":

> To See and Hear
> what is here,
> instead of what should be,
> was, or will be
>
> To Say
> what one feels and thinks
> instead of what one should
>
> To Feel
> what one feels,
> instead of what one ought
>
> To Ask
> for what one wants,
> instead of always waiting
> for permission
>
> To Take Risks
> on one's own behalf,
> instead of choosing only to be
> secure and not rock the boat.

She provided the tools to achieve these freedoms. This was a gift from her. I had always wanted to rock the boat, both for myself and for others, but these freedoms were very different from

---

The New Peoplemaking, p. 2 and p. 337.

the rebelliousness I had learned to survive. In the old country—
and in many countries today—if I rocked the boat by commenting
on what I heard and saw, if I said how I felt or what I wanted, I
would end up in jail or dead. To survive in that hierarchical
structure, we all had to learn to manipulate and be incongruent.
We had to deceive ourselves as well as others.

The Five Freedoms meant a lot to me, and my experience
was only one example of how strongly her work could touch
someone. Virginia's magic was how she made contact and
connected with people. Both stemmed from her valuing every
human being. As she connected with people, she saw them as
individual miracles and manifestations of life. As people felt her
deep validation of and respect for them, they responded with a
genuine valuing of themselves.

She looked for the gold in people. Rather than looking for
pathology or what was wrong with someone, she looked for the
strengths, the positives, and the possibilities. Therefore, no matter how negative a behavior seemed on the surface, she could
always discover its positive intent.

Because of my experiences during and after the war, I had
difficulty with the idea that there is gold in everyone. I felt angry
about the cruelty and inhumanity I had seen and endured. (Not
until much later did I accept the idea of discovering humanness
in everyone, without being judgmental. I learned that even people
who perform destructive acts are part of the human race.)

People have the potential for a range of good and evil. Virginia used to say, "We all have the potential of a Jesus Christ and
a Hitler in us. The question is how we use these." In other words,
each of us develops many parts, many inner resources. Some are
healthy and serve us well throughout life. Others no longer fit in
adulthood. Some become incongruent with how we feel, not in

line with our humanness. They are not right or wrong, good or bad. They once were useful and protected us. In growing up, for example, I had used my energy to please everybody. In wanting to be loved, it served me well to be a nice, good little girl. Now, as an adult, the healing process meant making new decisions about whether it was still useful for me. I needed to learn to say no sometimes.

Making contact on a deep level was Virginia's main effort. During the 1970 training, I heard rumors that she was thinking of bringing together a group of people whom she had reached in her various one-month workshops. Spending a week together in a beautiful environment would provide the opportunity to connect. We heard that she was going to do this for the first time after our workshop. People who were close to Virginia talked about going to Mexico. "What's this all about?" I asked my new friend Johanna, who was going.

"It's going to be called a Beautiful People conference. But, of course, it's only old friends who are invited."

The workshop near Minneapolis had been one of my best months ever. I wanted to learn more. Some wonderful people were there, and I also wanted to find out more about them. So I soon spoke to Virginia: "I hear that only people who are very special to you are invited to this place in Mexico."

"No," she said, "if you want to come, you can come. I just have to find out from my friend Bob whether there's enough room. Anyone who has taken one of my month-long workshops is invited."

Thrilled, I waited for the answer. I hadn't brought any extra money, my passport, or clothes with me that would be right for Mexico. So I didn't know how I was going to do this, but I was determined to go.

Virginia came back to say that yes, there was a bed for me. I phoned Paul, who had already come back from Europe and was expecting me to fly home. "I'm going to Mexico," I told him.

"What?!"

"I want to go to this conference, Paul. Please, could you send me some money and my passport?" He thought he had lost me. He could tell that I was determined to go, even if it meant breaking up our relationship. Still, he did everything I asked.

I went back to Minneapolis with a small group of those heading for Mexico. After buying summer clothes, we all boarded the plane for Mexico City. Then we traveled to a fantastic place, a paradise. Once the colonial-style palace of Hernan Cortez, it is now the Vista Hermosa Hotel, in Cuernavaca. We arrived at night, when everything was glistening and colorful. Beautiful lights shimmered all over the trees, and suddenly I could not figure out whether this was real. People who had arrived earlier were already having a party near the swimming pool, which had

Me with Virginia 1972

little Mayan statues in it. Virginia was standing there in a long dress.

"I don't know if I'll fit in," I thought. These people already knew each other. I only knew my fellow trainees. But I soon stopped worrying. It was a week of connecting, and I felt accepted. Some of the people there have since become my longest-term friends in the Satir group.

Every morning, the whole group got together to hear Virginia present her ideas. We did a lot of communication exercises to connect with each other. Having us assume various bodily stances and using what she called *sculptings*, Virginia's creativity offered the opportunity to understand and see ourselves and our relationships (internal and external) in a new way.

Experiencing these sculptings raised many questions for me, including: how do I protect myself? While we all protect ourselves and strive for acceptance in different ways, we build walls within ourselves and between others and ourselves. Meanwhile, we live on a socially acceptable survival level and perhaps acquire academic degrees, money, cars, and everything possible to be valued, respected, and loved in the world. What's missing is our reconnection with and acknowledgment of the self, the original life force, our feelings, vulnerabilities, and humanness. Being afraid to look inward or to reveal our authentic selves leads to emptiness, loneliness, and sometimes despair or other symptoms. Intimacy, real connection with another person, is based on sharing our vulnerabilities.

This healing process is a lifelong journey, she told us, and an unfolding process of body, mind, and spirit. Having all the resources we need, we can learn to be responsible. This means that none of our resources is in charge of us. We each are in charge of ourselves. We can use our resources with respect for others and for ourselves.

Among other things, I learned to practice congruence, a way of communicating without playing games. This was new to me. It meant saying what I was thinking and feeling, being true to my own feelings, and giving people feedback without judging them. It also meant taking responsibility for myself and letting others do the same. Again, I had to let go of the kind of loving control I'd learned in my family and in my country. Once I watched others being congruent and practiced it myself, however, I felt a new kind of freedom.

As mentioned, after we left Hungary, Paul and I decided not to belong to any religion. Keeping my Jewish background a secret became a conflict. Virginia once said not to confuse congruence with confession, so I struggled with this issue by myself.

The Satir model gave me a renewed resource for thinking: a roadmap to self-awareness, to choices, and to learning to use myself differently. She encouraged me to free myself from the rigidity of my professional training and the rules I had integrated. I learned that people are responsible themselves for their own growth, based on their readiness. The therapist simply provides the opportunity for them to make new choices, new decisions. Most importantly, I gave myself permission to trust my intuition, my values, my relationships, and myself.

Every afternoon and evening, we were on our own. From the first day, a large sheet of paper showed all the available rooms and places for people to sign up as presenters. They could talk about whatever they wanted to work on or to share. If someone just wanted to talk about any experience, we talked about that. So the program became our own, established after we got there, rather than being dictated to us ahead of time. I found this an interesting and exciting way to run a conference. It turned the week into an ongoing learning opportunity and an ongoing party.

At the same time, nobody had to do anything. If I wanted just to sit around the pool, I could do that. The idea was to get people connected in every possible way. I just loved it. By the end of the week, I was even more committed to learning and using Virginia's way of working with people. My whole journey made new sense to me. For me, meeting and working with Virginia satisfied all my earlier yearnings and dreams for freedom. Those dreams did come true. They were possible. People—including me—can be free, and we can find and free ourselves. I was not alone with my dreams. Other people believed that, too. I had found a community of like-minded people. I was sorry to leave at the end.*

---

* Fortunately, this group has met every year ever since then and has continued after Virginia's death in 1988. It is now called the International Human Learning Resource Network (IHLRN, pronounced "I learn"). Every third year, we go back to the original site in Mexico. The rest of the time, we meet somewhere else in the world. We can bring in friends, so this event has become a multicultural as well as international experience. I love going because all my friends are there and it's always a wonderful weeklong party.

Each friend represents a
world in us, a world possibly
not born until they arrive,
and it is only by this meeting
that a new world is born.
—*Anaïs Nin*

[I]f one advances confidently
in the direction of his
dreams, and endeavors to
live the life which he has
imagined, he will meet with
a success unexpected in
common hours.
—*Henry David Thoreau*

— *12* —

On the Edge

When I got home from the Beautiful People conference, Paul was not prepared for the changes in me. It was the first time I had gone away without him for five whole weeks. Somehow, I expected to have him instantly understand and join me in everything I'd just learned. This was a big mistake on my part.

Full of new awareness about having choices and creating a congruent relationship, I went around telling him how things were going to be different from then on. For instance, I declared, "I'm not going to be responsible for your food any more." Before the conference, my role had included controlling his diet. Then I had learned that if he wanted to eat improperly, it was his choice. "I am going to put things in the freezer, and you can take care of yourself. It's your responsibility."

Stunned and upset, he asked, "Do you still love me?"

"What am I doing?" I thought. Suddenly, my behavior seemed self-centered and inconsiderate rather than congruent. That experience taught me never to come home from a workshop like that. Unfortunately, the damage was done. Paul didn't even want to hear about Mexico, and he absolutely hated Virginia. He had this image of her as a social worker who grabbed people away. Despite my reassurances, he was really scared and saw her as his enemy and a threat. Whenever the training or the conference came up in conversation, he'd tell everyone, "I'm not afraid of Virginia Woolf." Then he'd say how awful things had become and how she'd changed me into a monster. I really resented these feelings of his because he didn't know Virginia and wouldn't even give her a chance.

I had already made plans go to another month-long workshop. It would be the following June in Colorado. When I told Paul, he said, "If you go, we will no longer be together. It's me or her." I wanted both, of course. Since I wasn't going to give up on my marriage, he'd have to meet Virginia. I knew that he would adore her.

Meanwhile, I kept telling him everything I felt. We had communicated like that before but not to the same extent. I actually became really rude in the process of practicing my new congruence, and he didn't know what was happening with me. He really thought I didn't love him any more. Yet, he tolerated me. Paul had a great deal of wisdom and patience. He was the kind of person who would look at me and say to himself, "Okay, she has changed. She'll settle down. I'll wait. I'll wait." It was true—I did settle down, eventually. Paul was usually right about things like that.

Early in 1971, a brochure arrived from a group of psychologists in Los Angeles who had invited Virginia to conduct a two-week workshop in Tahiti. The combined workshop and holiday trip would be in July, right after the Colorado workshop. Paul had always wanted to go to Tahiti, so I asked if he wanted to go in July. When he said yes, I told him, "Good, we'll go. Satir is going to be giving a workshop there."

"Well," he shrugged, "I'll be on the beach. I'm not going to the workshop. I don't care about Satir. But it's okay if you take the workshop." Paul accepted my going to Colorado because he would be going along to Tahiti. After the workshop, he and I met up in San Francisco and then flew down to join the group at the Los Angeles airport. When we arrived, I saw Virginia standing at the end of a long hallway in the airport. A tall, heavyset woman, she was dressed for Tahiti, wearing shorts, a tank top, and a ribbon in her hair. She looked like a huge little girl. When I pointed her out, Paul was amazed. He had imagined her as looking like a social work professor with big shoes, a tie, and a huge briefcase "That is Virginia?" he responded, his heart dropping into his stomach. A rapid shift was happening.

As we got closer, Virginia knew exactly how to break the ice. In Colorado, I had told her about Paul 's reaction to my going to her workshops. She wasted no time. "Paul," she said at once, "I understand that you hate me."

Paul didn't know what to do. She had confronted the biggest issue immediately. This, too, was completely different from all his internal pictures. Always very polite, he said, "Oh, no, Virginia. No, no."

"You don't have to placate me," Virginia said. "If I want to like you, I'll like you, and you can like me. So let's see what happens." After we got on the plane, Paul started taking Virginia coffee and tea. Totally fascinated, he did all he could do to look after her. In Tahiti, he didn't miss one second of the workshop. He told her, "I'm not interested in therapy, and I don't even understand half of what you are teaching." By the end, he had a good idea of what it was all about.

"I'm not interested in learning from you," he insisted to her. "I will never come to another workshop. But I want you to stay with us when you come to Manitoba, I want to see you and I want to love you." She had always dreamed of being loved for who she was and not for what she was doing, so they developed a

*Paul and Virginia
1973*

deep relationship. Paul cared for her very openly and was very straight with her. He was also protective and wanted to take care of her.

I always knew that Paul would love her, because she was who she was. Also, they both were very lovable and very special. So my plan worked, and I didn't have to choose between them. Indeed, Paul promised, "I'm going to support you in this." From then on, I didn't have any problem going to Virginia's work-shops. That year, Paul came with me to the Beautiful People conference, which was again in Vista Hermosa, Mexico. He loved it, and it became his most valued place and his group of people.

On May 1, 1971, Andy married Carol. They had met during his internship in internal medicine at a Winnipeg hospital where she was a nurse. They continued their relationship after Andy went to New York. Carol traveled through Europe, including Hungary, and they kept in touch despite their physical separa-tion. He met her in Paris, where they got engaged.

The wedding was in Winnipeg, and it was beautiful. We had a special Hungarian party at a friend's house, with a Hungarian smorgasbord and special cakes. My mother baked a chocolate cake especially for Andy (no one else was allowed to eat any). To prepare many special Hungarian dishes for the rest of us, she had cooked for weeks. We had music and champagne in the Hungarian way, as Paul wanted.

After the wedding in Winnipeg, Andy and Carol lived in New York until he finished his residency there in 1973. Before Andy started a six-month postgraduate internship in London, he and Carol participated in a month-long Satir workshop in Tacoma, Washington. Andy was very impressed with Virginia and the workshop. He and Carol also stopped in Winnipeg for a short time on their way to London. Carol often said that meeting our family and being with us was quite a new experience for her. With her family's Anglo-Saxon background, she'd grown up very differently. Our ways of relating and expressing feelings were somewhat strange for her.

While shopping one day in Winnipeg, I saw a ring I liked in a pawnshop window. I bought it for $10. Not long after, at a party, a man asked, "Where did you get that ring?"

"I bought it."

"Did you know that it is a Baha'i ring?" "No." I didn't know what that meant.

"This is really something very, very special," he explained, "and I want you to know about the Baha'i religion." That was his faith.

"I don't want to know about any religion. I'm not into any of that."

"What are you into?" he asked. I began telling him about Virginia Satir, and he became very interested in that. When I also told him about my planning background, he said, "We could really use some planning experience on the health services commission." He was the chairperson of that powerful board, which handled all funding for the province's health care system.

"I don't want to work for the government," I replied.

"Well, the commissioners only have to come to meetings, and we pay them for that time. I'm going to talk to the Minister of Health about you." The following week, that minister called, saying, "I understand that you know a lot about planning, and we need to learn about planning." We arranged to meet, and I thought about the possibility of adding this to my life.

Planning is very important in any country, but not to the extent that they did it in Hungary. When they adopted the Soviet system, they planned everything down to the smallest stores. This would be different, and therefore a new challenge. By the end of our meeting, the minister and I both had more information "Would you be willing to become a commissioner?" he asked.

"Not if it conflicts with my position at the hospital." Working in both positions might be a conflict of interest, as the commission approved all the hospital budgets. Hospitals in Manitoba were always struggling with their budgets, and the commission's yes or no to a proposal was like life or death. For example, to have another position allotted to my department, I first had to go through three different committees at the hospital; and when they approved my proposal, it was conditional on funding from the health services commission. "I'm not willing to leave my job," I added. "That's important for me."

The minister suggested that I talk with the president of St. Boniface. When I did, the president said, "Maria, it's a question of integrity. The only way you can do it is this. In the hospital, you will not be a commissioner; and on the commission, you will not be an employee of the hospital. You'll never tell me what's going on in the commission, and you won't attempt to represent this hospital when you're on the commission. Can you do that?"

"Of course. That's a challenge." I was curious to find out what was going on in the commission because I thought the health care system was in trouble. So I was appointed as a commissioner in much the same way I had ended up in the Planning Secretariat in Hungary—by fortunate coincidence. Things tend to happen to me this way in the world. They always have, and again, I think it's about being connected to something beyond me that guides my life.

During my term, I made two changes in my job at St. Boniface. First, I never asked for a raise. This was because my salary as the Director of Social Work was dependent on funds awarded by the commission. Second, I insisted on getting an assistant to deal with my department's budget. This kept me from being involved in any possibility or appearance of conflicting loyalties.

In 1972, Virginia invited trainees to join in her workshop in Natanya, Israel. Paul came along and, again, he just loved it. During that workshop, he became part of the group. He really understood and resonated with what he heard at the workshop. He also realized that he often got involved in his clients' family conflicts and situations because pets are family members, too. Sometimes, he recalled, one partner would bring the pet to be put to sleep. Often, it turned out, that request was related to some conflict in the relationship between partners. In other cases,

Paul thought it was the owner who needed the tranquilizer or medication, even though the pet was showing the symptom. Virginia encouraged Paul to write a book, and he began (but never finished) what he called "The Troubled Pet in the Family."

Following the workshop, we spent an additional week traveling in Israel. We both loved that country and found it fascinating. (Years later, in 2000, I went back with friends and thoroughly enjoyed being there again.)

Virginia normally taught groups of thirty to forty people who would then return to work in their respective organizations. Most of their supervisors didn't know the Satir approach to therapy, however, so it was difficult to use what they had learned and implement new ideas in their home environment. After the workshop in Colorado, I had told Virginia, "You really need to work on a systemic level. You need to teach throughout

Virginia Satir

organizations and systems—to teach supervisors and people in management positions—so that people who have been to your workshops can do their work." When she said she would like to do that, I asked, "Would you come to Manitoba for three months and try to work throughout the different systems?"

Given my work on Manitoba's health services commission, I knew this would be good for the province. Virginia might help us change the way we did things at all levels. To my complete surprise, she said, "Yes. I can come for September, October, and November of next year."

That was both wonderful and frightening. I didn't know how I would arrange it. How was I going to set up a three-month project, get approval, and get her paid? I would want people to have the chance to experience her regardless of whether they could afford it. Thinking I might find a way to make it a government project, so that people could participate regardless of their financial position, I got even more excited.

At the time, not many people knew who Virginia was. So I talked the idea through with the chair of the health services commission. I think he believed me because he experienced my enthusiasm and excitement for the project. At any rate, he went to see the Minister of Health. The minister had sufficient political savvy to see that this project looked progressive and inventive, so he agreed to arrange for the funding.

I suggested forming a committee to be responsible for the program's planning and implementation. Luckily, the chairperson turned out to be the university's Dean of Medicine, a powerful and excellent administrator. His committee included representatives from all the university faculties and administrators in the health field.

The plan was comprehensive and effective. For three months, Virginia worked on all levels of the health system and the social system: with government people, university faculties, profession-als, and patients, including children and their families. For the families, Virginia debuted what she called "Family Theaters," or "Lucy's 5-Cent Psychotherapy." We organized these first-ever workshops. In nine schools in different parts of Winnipeg and outside the city, children and parents could spend an evening with Virginia. In a fun way, they had the opportunity to learn about their communication and their family dynamics. This was so successful that on the last day of her three-month stay, the government arranged a Family Theater at the Manitoba Theatre Centre. It was so full that many people couldn't get in. That was the families' goodbye to Virginia.

Before that, we had organized a two-week training on family therapy. We invited select people from all helping professions in the province. Every day, Virginia did live family interviews. She also spent three days at the University of Manitoba, teaching communication to all faculties, including the faculty of medicine.

The president of St. Boniface Hospital loved Virginia and invited her to do a weeklong workshop on communication for the entire hospital staff. She agreed, but it took some logistical thinking to get it all planned for a week, since the hospital had to keep operating. Everyone at St. Boniface—from the cleaning staff to heads of departments—participated. Virginia worked from morning until midnight. In the hospital's auditorium, she set up groups of four people to discuss a topic together. Each group con-sisted of a physician, an administrator, a maintenance person, and another health professional. For the most part, this meant that they had to connect with people they did not know and usually would not talk to.

One day, Virginia asked, "Who here has ever had anything to do with the president of the hospital?" He was a very popular person, but no one actually recognized him when he walked around the place. During the workshop, he was always in the background. So she told me, "Maria bring him down right away." When he got to the stage, she turned him around and told the audience, "This is your president." Turning to him, she continued, "You had better go around and talk to people in this hospital, because we all have to learn about communication." She did all this in a very loving way.

Being on the health services commission, I also introduced Virginia to people in the government. My Baha'i friend was totally taken by her, so he organized an evening with the most important hospital administrators, physicians, and government people in the health services. Virginia called it the White Paper Group because she had seen a white paper with suggestions about how Manitoba's health system might operate. These people came when the head commissioner invited them but, having very different ideas about public health issues, they had difficulty communicating with each other. At the time, there was a lot of conflict between the hospitals, the doctors, and the government, which paid them all. The meeting's purpose was to provide an opportunity for them to communicate and to find ways to work together to build a better system for delivering health services.

Once again, Virginia made up small groups of people who had never talked to each other: one civil servant, one hospital administrator, one doctor, and one government person. Then she said, "You all have a dream about health care in Manitoba. I'm sure that everybody here has his own dream. Now, I want you to talk to each other about that dream." Once they had a dialogue, these people discovered that their dreams were very similar. What differed was their ways of realizing the dream. This was a tremendous new awareness.

After that session, the Minister of Health called us in for a meeting. He wanted to set up a dinner with the premier of the province, some other high-level officials, and Virginia. The intent was to discuss some interpersonal conflicts. Virginia said she would do this on the condition that he didn't expect her to be on anyone's side. I thought she showed tremendous integrity in laying down the rules and boundaries to the person who footed the bill.

She told me she was worried about the meeting. She had all the information I had about the current issues, but she had never conducted anything on that level. I wasn't going to attend, but on the appointed day, we went an hour early to look over the room at the hotel where the meeting was to take place. It was set up very blandly, like a government regulation dinner. "Maria," she said, "get hold of some candles and flowers. I can't work in this room." I rushed around to find everything. After we set it up, she said, "I'm afraid. I don't know what the hell I'm going to go do."

"I'm afraid, too." It was almost time for the others to arrive, so I left her there.

The purpose of life, after all,
is to live it, to taste the
experience to the utmost, to
reach out eagerly and
without fear for newer and
richer experience.

—*Eleanor Roosevelt*

When she got home at 11 that evening, she exclaimed, "Oh, it was great!"

"What did you do?"

"I just treated them symbolically as if they were a family. There was papa with his two sons, and they had a problem. Then there were the two grandsons. Altogether, the kinds of problems they had were called government issues. But when I dealt with them as family issues and family processes, they all understood what was going on. There was a lot of jealousy and a lot of competition, stress, and all that. And everything got resolved." Within the government structure, the processes and feelings were just like those in a family. Only the issues—the content—differed. On any administrative level, Virginia could identify feelings such as competition, protectiveness, striving for achievement, jealousy, and wanting distance or closeness. "The family is a microcosm of the world," she used to say.

These experiences showed me that the Satir family systems theory can be used on and among all levels of any group. It doesn't matter whether the organization is a family, a government, or a nation. While this had been the first time Virginia worked at that level, she soon followed this experience by doing the same thing in Sweden.

At the start of those three months in Manitoba, she stayed in our house awhile before getting her own apartment. That was when Paul got to be one of her very close friends. He appreciated her qualities and her work, but he also tried to protect her from doing too much. Telling me, "She works too hard," he'd fuss over her. Virginia called him Papa and treated him as a surrogate father, in a way. Again, what she really loved in Paul was that he did not love her for being a therapist or because she was famous. He often said he loved her for herself, for being a human being.

She never did therapy with us—he would have objected to that—but she often made comments about our being enmeshed with each other and how we communicated. Over the years, we eventually learned how to live together without placating and how to respect our differences. Our relationship was very Hungarian: loving and hating each other passionately at the same time. We had different interests, and we learned how to keep our individual preferences and autonomy while simultaneously being connected on a profound level. Our relationship deepened over the years.

At first, Virginia was my mentor and I put her on a pedestal (she, of course, wanted very much to step down from there). I idealized her. Later, I also knew her little-girl vulnerabilities from her own past. The nice thing was that she was so human. She often talked about her loneliness and her limitations. She thought she was not attractive enough to find an intimate relationship with a man, yet she always hoped that a shining knight on a white horse would appear.

Virginia was married and divorced twice. Once during a workshop, someone challenged her: "How can you teach family therapy when you've been divorced twice?"

"That's how I learned it," she responded. However, she also told me that in both marriages, she realized that her husbands had wanted her to act like a mother and had wanted to be dependent on her. Another time, when we were on a cruise together, she said she would like to go to a gardening workshop. There she would find a man who would be interested in her as a person, not as a therapist or for what she carried with her name. Her wish was to be loved for herself.

Another time, we spent a few days in Hawaii after a conference. We were in a big house on the beach that someone had provided for her. I liked being on the beach in the sun, and she loved being in the kitchen. She cooked wonderful chicken soup and rhubarb pie. I cherished these times we spent together after workshops or conferences.

Through these experiences, I learned to know her as a human being, as a person, and as a woman. It didn't take away from seeing her as a genius, which she was. At other times, I experienced her being very tough, demanding, and critical. She had very high expectations of people close to her. We talked about being "in the doghouse," and we used to keep track of who was in or out of the doghouse. This was helpful in that it showed her humanness and brought her down from the pedestal.

Wherever we went, we visited all the nurseries. She loved flowers. We also went to the tall-girl shops. She was very careful about spending money, however. I often wondered why she had to be so careful. After her death, we found out that she had a large estate, which she left for the Avanta organization. Still affected by growing up in the Depression, she had learned that money must be saved in case hard times come along.

Virginia had two families. One was her family of origin and her two adopted children. The other was the family she chose: her friends and colleagues. She often talked about her brothers, her sister, and her two adopted daughters. Her growing up had been difficult at times but, as a friend of ours commented, "If Virginia had had an ideal life in her growing up, she wouldn't be the family therapist that she is."

I absolutely agree that some of the negative things that happen to us later become our assets. Like Virginia's, my interest in families came from my own experiences. If I hadn't felt so powerless with my cousins during those summers as a child, maybe I wouldn't have rebelled as much —or survived—the way I did.

After 1973, my mother's health was not good. Although she had done extremely well after her brain surgery a decade earlier, she started having many accidents and was often hospitalized after 1973. Once, she broke her hip; another time, her leg. We assumed her brain tumor had recurred, but she didn't want to know about it. She liked to be in the hospital because I worked there, and I often teased her about breaking her bones to get back to the orthopedic ward.

Paul, too, had some serious health problems. Years before, in Toronto, he had caught the flu and then developed bronchitis. As we had no money and no contacts, he did not get proper treatment. In the end, he developed an asthma condition. Then, in Jamaica in 1964, during our first holiday since moving to Canada, he experienced chest pain and a shortness of breath. We hoped these were due to the sudden heat. On our way home, however, we stopped in Toronto to see a physician friend. He diagnosed angina and suggested that Paul admit himself to a hospital immediately upon arriving in Winnipeg. In those days, the prescribed treatment was to rest for three weeks. Paul rested in

My mother
1969

the hospital during the day, but he sneaked out at night to work in his veterinary clinic.

By the end of 1973, Paul's heart condition worsened. Three arteries were clogged, so his cardiologist hospitalized him for tests and recommended open-heart surgery. This was a very difficult time for us. We knew that the surgery was a critical intervention that might save his life, but it was also a great risk.

Paul had a hard decision to make. He lived passionately and enjoyed every moment. He had always said, "I don't want to be disabled. I don't want to lose any of my senses. I don't want you to take care of me. I want to live until I cannot live with quality of life." Loving his work, people, and music, he believed that he had an acceptable quality of life. His goal was always "to give life to the years, not years to life." And he did.

His cardiologist did not agree. He gave him six months to live without the surgery and another five years with it. In March, Andy and Carol flew back from London to support Paul through his hospital stay. Andy was instrumental in helping Paul make his decision. After seeing Paul's X-rays, he encouraged him to have the surgery. Eventually, Paul agreed. On his surgeon's request, he lost forty pounds in preparation for the May 1974 operation.

Andy was a great support for me, too. I was terrified. I knew that the surgery was the best way to proceed. I also knew the risk involved. The terrible experience of my father's death just before surgery was shadowing my fears as well. As I had done so many times in my life, I was facing another very painful, frightening possibility. I saw myself being on the edge of a cliff, looking down into a void and being full of fear.

The day before the surgery, in May, Virginia came to see Paul. He said later that she told him, "Just keep one thing in mind and hear my voice saying: 'Breathe.'" He did.

When she left early the next day, she told me, "I'll be back when Paul comes home." The open-heart surgery was successful, and she phoned daily during Paul's two-week hospital stay to see how he was doing. In the recovery room, he was hooked up to all kinds of tubes and machines. For the few minutes we were allowed to visit, all I could see were his eyes. At least they were alive.

When Andy went to pick up Paul's glasses after the operation, the head nurse gave him a letter as well. Paul had written it before the surgery, to be given to us only if he died. We read it anyway, and we were moved. Paul expressed his love for us, especially to Andy, who had come home to share time and to tell Paul in person how much he loved him. Another part was about people in his clinic: he wanted us to get his nurse another job, if he died. He also instructed us to have a party rather than a funeral. Since he had had such an enriching and loving life, we should celebrate his life. This letter is still very precious to us.

Each day of recovery was a risk, which made it a very hard time. Fortunately, Paul had the best medical care, and we had lots of support. He was discharged two weeks after the surgery. I was surprised when Virginia actually came back after his release, knowing how busy she was. After her three months in Manitoba in 1972, she often came back to work with many different groups, from aboriginal people to professionals to parents and children. In 1974, I also organized one of her international workshops in Manitoba. So I knew how extremely full her schedule was that year.

When she saw my surprise, she said, "You still don't trust me. I came to say goodbye to Paul before the operation because I knew he would live, and I can only say hello after I've said goodbye." She took Paul on a walk to the zoo. It was heaven for him, as he adored her and knew what it meant that she'd taken a day off from a workshop to fly back to see him.

In many ways, the concept of trust had been killed in me during my life in Hungary. There were very few people whom I could really trust and continue to trust. They were very valuable for me, but I also got burned by some. It took a while to learn to trust. In general, I still don't have perfect judgment about who to trust, but the difference now is that I get the real picture much sooner.

My committed relationships go beyond trust. I trust those people and would protect them no matter what they do. If they didn't live up to my expectations, it would not matter. That's important for me. However, I am committed to loving them. I would do anything for them. I can count on them. They can count on me. It's based on experience.

Trusting people was different for Paul. Nobody could ever disappoint Paul, because he trusted people beyond their behavior. He often quoted the saying, "A stranger is a friend I haven't met yet." Beyond family, I feel very fortunate having a few friends in my life now whom I love and trust. I think it's loving that makes the difference. That's more than trusting.

Coming back to be with Paul precipitated a big change in Andy's plans. He decided to stay in Winnipeg for his fellowship exams. As proud as I was of Andy's professional progress during his time away, I was happy to have him back. Later, when Carol became pregnant with their first child, little Paul, they decided to stay beyond the exams. Andy had his belongings shipped home from New York, where he had left them during his time in England.

The period after Paul's surgery continued being very stressful for me. While he had been recuperating on one hospital ward, my mother had been on another. After Paul's release, my mother had to be hospitalized again and again with broken bones and generally deteriorating health. She could no longer live alone anymore, even though we were in the same apartment building. Then, on January 5, 1975, she died from pneumonia in St. Boniface Hospital. I believe she was ready to go, but I regret that she never saw Andy's children.

I learned to respect my mother in the last years of her life. She adjusted very well to living in Canada, even though she did not know the language. When she reluctantly moved to her own apartment, she again adjusted very well. After a while, she said that it was the best idea Paul had ever had, because she became more autonomous. She developed friendships, played bridge, cooked, and never complained.

When they discovered her brain tumor, her left side was already paralyzed and her surgeon said the operation would not change that. After the surgery, she exercised that left hand and arm nonstop. She had such will power. Miraculously, she regained movement on her left side to the extent that her surgeon presented her case at a hospital conference as an unusual recovery. To attend that conference, she bought a wig and requested a German translator. She was very proud of herself, and I was proud of her, too. After the conference, someone asked her, "Do you have a wish?"

"Yes," she said with a smile, "I'd like to be fifty years younger and marry my neurosurgeon." She adored him.

I think she was eighty-six when she died, but she never told us her age. The only time she talked about it was five years after she came to Canada, when she found out that she was eligible for an old age pension at age sixty-five.

I realize now how much I got from her: my strong will, my courage, and my ability to adjust to new situations. I'm grateful that I had an opportunity later in her life to connect with her as a person and to learn to respect her.

On April 23, 1975, Andy's son Paul was born. I knew I was going to have a grandchild but had no idea what this meant. From the moment little Paul was born, our life changed. It was a great gift to have so much time with him. He stayed with us many times and even had his own room and crib in our apartment. For my husband Paul, it was very special to see this baby growing up. Since he had missed the first two and a half years of Andy's life, little Paul became his major focus and source of happiness. They spent lots of time together, and he devised games to play together. They listened to music and, when he was four, Paul looked at his grandfather and said, "Papa, you are my best friend." We both cherished every moment we spent with him. For me, Paul has been a very special person ever since he was born. I believe he is an old soul and that we have had many lives together.*

*Me with
Andy's son Paul
1979*

*Me, Paul, and
Andy's son Paul
1976*

Meanwhile, in May 1975, in the middle of a staff meeting, I got so sick that I couldn't even drive myself home. For the next few days, I had nausea, dizziness, and diarrhea. I was so dehydrated after a few days that I ended up in the hospital, where my doctor diagnosed acute colitis. I stayed in the hospital for over two months. My doctor advised surgery, which terrified me in general. I especially resisted it in this area of my body. Beyond that, my intuition told me not to have this operation. Eventually, my doctor discharged me on a heavy dose of cortisone.

I was very weak, and taking the cortisone was the only way I could survive, but I suffered the side effect of becoming extremely dejected. My life was okay in every other respect, so I couldn't understand the extent of my depression, which frequently

---

* As I write this, he is in his mid twenties, and I am very proud to have him in my life and to be his grandmother. He has a heart of gold, a brilliant mind, and a shining spirit. We have a great relationship as friends.

led to suicidal ideas. These seemed totally unrelated to anything else that was going on in my life. By September, I was still so weak that I could only work part time at St. Boniface. It was hard to make it through half a day, which was very unusual for me.

A year earlier, in June 1974, Winnipeg's social work association had invited a psychiatrist to speak about group homes. I usually didn't attend these boring annual meetings, but my friend Beverley told me not to miss this man, Dr. Ben Wong. She said he was a very interesting speaker. I was curious enough to attend the lecture, planning to stay for an hour. As I listened, though, I kept staying longer and longer. I ended up being glued to my chair for the whole day.

He didn't talk about group homes, he talked about energy and all kinds of stuff that I'd never heard about. As usual, I was curious to find out more. One of my special interests was to invite exceptional educators—such as Yetta Bernhard, Bunny and Fred Duhl, and others—to share their ideas with our community. I love sharing my learnings, ideas, and friends. Connecting people is my passion. To organize these events, some of my interested friends (including Eleanor Adaskin) and I soon formed a nonprofit organization, Professional Education, Inc. So, at the end of Dr. Wong's presentation, I asked whether he would come and talk to the St. Boniface staff. He agreed to a date in October 1975, saying he would also bring his partner, Dr. Jock McKeen.

That date happened to be shortly after I went back to work after being in the hospital. My curiosity compelled me to attend but, still being very fragile, I intended to listen only. The first day was a total surprise for me, not at all what I expected. It was about bodywork, which I had never seen or experienced. I knew nothing about bioenergetics. As I watched them working with one of my colleagues, I thought, "There must be a better way to do therapy than this." This staff member, who was dealing with his anger, was screaming as they pushed the life out of him and stuck acupuncture needles into him. I thought, "What are they doing to this man? I never should have brought them here." I felt very confused.

The next day, I was in charge of getting them to the hospital from their hotel downtown. To my great surprise, as we drove, I heard them say, "We were talking about you last night."

I hadn't said one word the previous day, so I was amazed that they'd even noticed me. "What did you talk about?"

"We want to help you and work with you today, because we can see that you are falling apart. You are dying inside."

I was horrified, and all my suspiciousness and skepticism from the past came back to me. "Nobody can help me," I said, "and definitely you cannot, with this approach that you use. Yes, I am falling apart. I can hardly pull myself together. But I don't need that kind of treatment."

However, no matter what I said during that ten-minute car ride to the hospital, they insisted that they wanted to help me. So I agreed, but I said I did not want them to touch me, I didn't want to take my clothes off, I didn't want any acupuncture needles, and I didn't want to talk. I really didn't want these dangerous things to happen to me. And I hoped that, with all these conditions, they would get discouraged and give up. They didn't.

When the morning meeting began, I heard one of them say, "We will work with Maria now." Then they reassured me that the contract stood: no touching, no needles, nothing that I had seen the day before. The only thing I had to do was to breathe. "Well," I thought, "this is rather safe. Breathing can't hurt."

Obviously, I had no idea where breathing could take me. In the following hour and a half, I experienced something I did not know existed. As I followed their directions about how to breathe, I heard myself saying things on the outside that were coming from the inside. I heard words and statements that were not coming from my head, but from the deep core of my being. I experienced tears and sobbing from the inside, and I didn't know why I was crying. I heard myself saying that I deserved to kill myself, if not with the colitis, then with the cortisone.

I got in touch with an unresolved guilt over my mother's death, something I had never been conscious of. The words that came from an unconscious level indicated that I thought I should have done more, I wasn't good enough, I should have kept her alive. I should have done more and more for her. I blamed myself for her death and hated myself for her suffering, This guilt and self-hate created my symptoms and illness, I believe.

Ben and Jock were very respectful. They were loving, and they were caring. As I was making connections between my actions, my perceptions, my own interpretations, and consequently my life, I became aware that I was in charge of making new choices about the consequences. This was a turning point in many ways. As soon as I understood the connection between my symptoms and my unconscious guilt and self-hate, I knew I could deal with it. I decided to let the guilt go and to take charge of the symptoms and the illness. On a conscious level, I knew that I could not have done more for her. I took myself off the cortisone slowly, knowing that I didn't need it any more. The healing process took its turn, and I've never suffered from colitis since then, in spite of all the medical predictions.

Each time I survived being on the edge, in spite of expecting disaster or wanting to die from the anxiety, pain, and fear. My experiences than became something to learn from. I believe in myself and in the unfolding process of living.

I learned from my experience with Ben and Jock to search for the deep core issues and to understand the interpretations that I make to keep them out of awareness. I knew and had learned much about the unconscious before, but only theoretically. I had never experienced it on that deep level in my soul and body. I had known in theory that symptoms relate to stress, but this was a real experience. I learned that beyond my consciousness, there was a whole life, a whole field, and a whole range of physical harm that I could inflict on myself. There was a voice that came from my guts, and there was a me that was beyond my head. That was my experience from this bodywork. I felt drawn to their work in a similar yet very different way from what I experienced with Virginia. I wanted to learn more about what these guys were teaching and doing—and I have been learning ever since.

Since that first Winnipeg experience, I've been to many of their programs and seminars. During my first time at a Come Alive workshop, on Cortez Island in 1975, I learned something I'd never expected. When I got there, I did not like the accom- modations, so I decided to leave after the first day. When I shared my plan in the group, Ben told me in very definite terms that I had to stay. He was the first person who'd ever stood up to me that way, and I was terribly angry. Rebellious as ever, I wanted to run away. However, there was no transportation from this island. Reluctantly, I stayed, as an observer sitting outside the group. After a few days, I wished to participate, but I did not.

At the workshop's end, they had a party. Ben offered to read my Tarot cards. I felt shame. I had behaved like shit, and he was offering me a gift. I became more curious and fascinated by these guys. I respected them, and I wanted to learn more.

After that, we met almost every year when they came to do Come Alive workshops in Winnipeg. I admire their humanness, their knowledge, and their dealing with people with such great respect and responsibility. Over the years, we developed a great friendship. I cherish it, and I appreciate everything I've learned from them. My work with people and my way of living reflect these learnings. It's compatible with Satir's work and with everything else that I believe in and have ever learned.

When Ben and Jock announced a five-day workshop in Winnipeg for Spring 1979, Paul told me, "I want to go to this workshop and really get to know these two guys. I want to have my own thing with them, so you can't come. I don't want to be Mr. Maria Gomori."

Although Paul wasn't a workshop person, he enjoyed their Come Alive workshop and getting to know Ben and Jock. They integrated all sorts of therapy—including acupuncture, bodywork, and music—into this experience. Participants got all kinds of opportunities to experience themselves, to find out who they were, and to learn new ways to communicate. Healing was taking place on levels of body, mind, and spirit. As a result, people were making very important new choices for their lives. I felt grateful that Paul was choosing to participate.

Paul loved the music that followed every part of the work. Later, Ben and Jock told me that after each piece of music, Paul would say something to make it light. That was his way—to transform heaviness into lightness. He also got in touch with Ben and Jock's art of healing and their humanity. When he came home, he said, "Now I really understand why you love these people and what they are doing. I don't want to go to any more workshops. I understand it now." He had made a wonderful connection with them, and they with him.

Meanwhile, a year after meeting Ben and Jock, I had the opportunity to connect them with Virginia. The Association for Humanistic Psychology was holding a conference on a cruise ship. For once, Virginia came as a participant. It was a holiday for her. Ben and Jock were also at the conference, so they met her and hit it off.

At their request, she led a three-week workshop in 1982 on Quadra Island. From then on, she taught twice a year at "The Haven," their beautiful resort and educational center for Personal Development seminars, on Gabriola Island in British Columbia. That spot became my second home, and Virginia used to say that she loved being and working there. It was the most nurturing and high-energy place she'd experienced.*

She loved Ben and Jock. They questioned one another's ideas, gave feedback, and were both loving and critical. Ben and Jock challenged Virginia's beliefs on change and hope, talking instead about transformation and faith. I always enjoyed listening to their discussions. They all had a lot of respect for each other, on both a professional and personal level.

Ben, Jock, and Virginia on Cortez Island
1982

Ben and Jock invited me to participate in all of Virginia's workshops on Gabriola Island. Twice a year from 1983 to 1988, she gave three-week workshops there. These were tremendous learning opportunities for me. Every day, I got to discuss her work with her. I'd ask about what the thinking had been behind her interventions and how she had reached certain conclusions. She worked intuitively, so the process wasn't always clear. She didn't sit down and give people instructions about how to work. If you asked her a question, however, she'd explain, "Oh, yeah, this is what was in my mind, and this is how I was processing it."

This was the first time I had the time and the relationship with her that let me take advantage of this opportunity. Having three weeks with her on Gabriola twice a year for five years helped me find out much more about the process and how she used her creativity.

---

* Ben and Jock named one of The Haven's recreation rooms "The Satir Room." In the garden, a sculpture in her memory now stands surrounded by beautiful flowers.

Physical strength can never permanently withstand the impact of spiritual force.

—*Franklin Roosevelt*

There are times when we must sink to the bottom of our misery to understand truth, just as we must descend to the bottom of a well to see the stars in broad daylight.

—*Vaclav Havel*

— *13* —

Transitions

In 1977, I told Virginia that I wanted to be her intern. She'd never had interns, but I felt it would be a perfect way for me to move to the next level of learning. When I asked again in 1978, she agreed: "Oh, that would be wonderful, because next year, I'm going to do a month-long workshop in Germany, near Frankfurt."

"No, no!" I exclaimed. I'd already told her my feelings about Germany, and she'd told me I had to work on this. At the time, I had had no intention or interest. "Take me somewhere else," I told her.

"Well, that's the workshop where I want you to intern." She was giving workshops in lots of other countries, but she only offered me the choice of being an intern in Germany.

"I'd rather die." That was the end of that conversation, for the time being. A year later, in 1978, Paul and I went to the annual Avanta meeting in Aspen, Colorado. While he liked going to the annual meetings and other gatherings, he still preferred to do his own thing rather than participate. Virginia and I had lunch together. "Well," she asked, "are you coming with me to Germany?" The workshop was in July 1979.

"Why do you want me to go there? Because you want me to change my opinion?"

"No, I really would like to have your support over there. I've never been to Germany. I've been invited year after year, for many years, and now I believe that all my theories and my concepts about people would go down the drain if I also believed there are millions of people in this world who cannot change because they happen to be German.

"I've been ashamed about what went on in Germany," she continued, "because my ancestors were German. That's one of the reasons I've refused to go till now. We'll buy open-return tickets, and if we don't like it, we'll leave."

It was a relief that she wasn't trying to change me. My attraction to Virginia was due to her belief system. The one thing that I questioned—and still question—was her conviction that all people are basically good. I can say "Maybe" to that, but she really believed it. When I think about this, a story comes to my mind. Thousands of years ago, the big gods had a debate. They wanted people to have a soul but didn't want to make it obvious. One said: "Take it to the moon. Nobody will find it." Another said: "Put it in the lakes." After a long discussion, they came to an agreement. "Let's put it inside people. They will have to look inside themselves to find it." Some people looked. One of them was Virginia. As she wrote,

> It was as if I saw through the inner core of each being, seeing the shining light of the spirit trapped in a thick black cylinder of limitations and self-rejection. My effort was to enable the person to see what I saw. Then, together, we could turn the dark cylinder into a large, lighted screen and build new possibilities.*

We had had lots of discussions about that, and she was able to find good in everyone. She would dismiss any signs of evil in a person. I even saw her doing that with people who were evil

---

* *The New Peoplemaking*, pp. 340–41.

with her. However, my experiences in life had been very different from hers.

At lunch, I told her, "If you want me to go to Germany because you want my support, then I'll go."

"Oh, no, I don't want your support. I want your partnership."

That changed the context for me. We knew what we were getting into, and would do it together, as a team. We both wanted to learn.

By July, however, Paul was suffering from severe asthma attacks. His condition had been getting worse since 1978, and now he was having difficulty controlling it. He often became unconscious during an attack. A few times, he had to go to the hospital emergency room to get oxygen.

The previous year, his doctor had advised him to cut back to part-time work. On that schedule, unfortunately, he could not keep up with the clinic's expenses. So he made some attempts to find a partner. That didn't work out. Instead, he decided to sell his clinic in 1978. He pretended to enjoy his retirement, but I think he missed the work and his patients. His asthma worsened.

I was afraid to leave him to join Virginia, but he kept pushing me to go without him. "You really need to go back to Germany. You're caught up in these feelings about Germans, and you have to experience them differently. Go with Virginia. I want you to learn more."

I phoned her, saying, "I cannot leave Paul for all four weeks right now. I can only make it for two weeks. Is that okay?" She told me it was. I had hoped for the opposite answer, since participating and being on time were important expectations of hers.

I still felt hostile when I left for Germany. I was going into a workshop with a group of people I didn't want to be around. I had told Paul that I would be happy if I found just one human being among the sixty-five German people in the group.

Changing planes in Amsterdam, I learned that the flight on which I was booked had been canceled. I had to take a Lufthansa flight instead. This was a problem. Virginia was sending somebody to pick me up in Frankfurt, but now I was on a different plane and didn't know how to get hold of her. I knew she was holding the workshop somewhere in the mountains, but I didn't know where.

Fortunately, when I arrived in Frankfurt, the woman who picked me up had already found out about my new flight. When I told her how impressed I was with her finding me under the circumstances, she said, "Don't forget that you are in Germany, and we are perfectly organized."

That was the first statement I heard in Germany, and it was spoken by the first German person I'd met since the war. "Here I am again," I thought bitterly, "among the most wonderfully organized and perfect people in the world." On the way up to the workshop, I tried to find out what had happened in the first two weeks. She wouldn't tell me anything, explaining that she was only there to drive me.

We arrived at the place while the group was in the middle of a break. During Virginia's breaks, people were always dancing. When I walked in, Virginia started to dance with me. Everybody knew that I had arrived. After the dancing, Virginia introduced me to the group of about sixty people. Then, ten minutes later, she announced that she would randomly split them into two groups each afternoon to do Family Reconstructions. I'd work with one group in this room while Virginia worked with the second group in another room.

My heart stopped. I had never conducted a Family Reconstruction—the most complex process in the Satir model—let alone with a strange group in Germany. I had planned just to be an intern, to observe and learn. I knew that German people want everything to be perfect, and I was not perfect. That evening, over dinner, I told Virginia, "I am not going to do this."

"Why do you think you're here?" she started. "You wanted to be an intern."

"But I've never done a Family Reconstruction."

"You have to start sometime, and I'm right here."

"That's part of the problem," I said. "You're here in the very next room, and nobody will want to have anything to do with me. Everybody will want to work with you." When I could not convince her to change her mind, I told myself, "I never should have come." More memories of the war came back to me, and I knew I was going to fail in front of Virginia and in front of all these people. I had a sleepless night.

The next morning, I walked into the lion's den. After Virginia randomly selected the two groups, I began my first reconstruction. I had the advantage of knowing German, which meant that participants in my group could work in their own language. Things moved well, and I realized that I knew much more than I thought I knew. Amazed, I saw that the process Virginia had taught was working for me, as well. As long as I followed the process, it led me to where we needed to go.

Family Reconstruction is all about recreating the context of past learnings and providing an opportunity for new choices and transformation. To figure out where a person's core issues lay, I had to go through each step carefully. I spent hours with people to get their life stories (Virginia didn't need detailed stories). Along with these, I'd study the star's Family Map, which is like a family tree with descriptive information. Then I'd make a design about where to start. This was at night, after six or seven hours of doing the previous reconstruction. Then, the next morning over coffee with Virginia—the only time we had to discuss issues from my group—I'd go over everything with her.

In just five minutes, she'd tell me where the main issue was, where the conflict was, and where the transformation had to take place. It was amazing to see how her mind worked—and how fast. Each evening between 7 and 10 o'clock, she'd complete a Family Reconstruction. It sometimes took me until 3 in the morning to finish one. But she was right—this was the way to learn it. Step by step.

I realize now that life and learning is a process not only of asking questions and collecting answers. More importantly, it means having the courage to explore the mysteries and the forces that are shaping the world and us. Often, our old assumptions no longer hold true.

One of the people I worked with was ashamed and angry about his father, who was very cruel and had worked in the SS. Transformation means making new decisions, new choices, and letting go of whatever does not fit anymore. But this participant wouldn't even look at or talk to the person who played the role of his father in the reconstruction. As a result, I had to abandon the whole process.

A few days later, I was working with a woman whose father had also been very cruel. He'd come home and slap the faces of his wife and three daughters. Without knowing about the man with the SS father (she had been in Virginia's group in the other room during his reconstruction), she chose him to play the part of her own father. When we got to the scene where the father comes home, this young man ran into the room and threw this woman up against the wall. Instantly, I told people to freeze where they were.

Shaking, the young man said, "I don't have to work any longer on understanding my father." After despising him for his inhumanity, the son had now seen his own capacity for cruelty. The opportunity to play a brutal man led him to an awareness of his own potential for being cruel. We had arrived at the moment of transformation. He had the same resources as his father, and once he became aware of this, he recognized and owned it. He no longer judged his father as he had before. Rather, he could identify and separate. He realized that he had the choice about using his resources differently.

Over and over again, amazing things happened in this workshop. Somehow, people chose role-players who always fit. I know now that there are no accidents. This process is a spiritual experience, and we are all connected on a deep level. As Virginia put it, "Each of us emerges as a bud on a universal spiritual tree. That tree links all human beings through its roots."

Gradually, I became aware that, even though most of the participants had been born during or after the war, I had been criticizing and blaming them for the past. I felt ashamed for not thinking about this already, knowing that I wouldn't want Andy to be hated for anything that I had done. I had been blaming these people for the past. Now I was seeing them as human beings with feelings.

Another afternoon, I worked with a Jewish woman who was originally from Prague. The Nazis had deported her father and her to Auschwitz when she was thirteen. (She was an only child, and her mother had not been Jewish.) Her father died in a gas chamber. Now, she wanted to connect with him again and to say goodbye to him.

This was too loaded for me, so I told her to do the reconstruction with Virginia. After agreeing to do it, Virginia sent us away to work on the Family Map. When we returned, Virginia said, "Maria is going to do the reconstruction, after all."

It was a terrible task and challenge. I didn't want to revisit Auschwitz, not even in a reconstruction. But I knew I had to do it. Virginia gave me only one statement to work with: "Your star wants to say goodbye to her father. Don't forget you cannot say goodbye to somebody you haven't said hello to." That statement contained a whole lecture. The message was that I had to start at the beginning, when the star had been a child and meeting her father. Unfortunately, she had totally blocked any recollections of her childhood. Her earliest memories were of being in the concentration camp.

The woman was allowed to choose twenty people to participate that afternoon—which meant that the other forty might think she didn't trust them. As echoes of the anti-Semitic past rippled through the air briefly, she considered who would play the part of her father. The man she chose was also from Czechoslovakia and was the person who later started the international family therapy movement in Europe. She went on to choose the players for the drama: Germans to play Nazis, a woman to play her mother, and so on.

Once we started the reconstruction, something shifted. When we sculpted her mom and dad, she started to remember picnics and other events of her early years. She went on to describe a lovely family, and she did feel reconnected with her father. The man who played that role often spoke Czech to her during these scenes. It was beautiful to watch her face as they all reenacted her childhood memories.

As we went through the whole story, some of the German participants played the Nazis who took them to the concentration camp. One even played Dr. Josef Mengele at the Auschwitz train stop, signaling for her father to go to the right—to his death—while she went to the left. Then we had a scene in which her father talked to her from wherever he exists now. Again, she felt the connection she had hoped to feel.

The participants all played their roles in the most human manner, with realism and sincerity. We all—actors and observers—felt as if we were in a trance, really living through these stories. When we talked about the whole thing afterward, many people said they wanted to die. They felt they could not live with what had happened. Looking out the window at the darkened German landscape, I said, "Nowhere else in the world would people understand what this was about, or even role-play it so well." The paradox impressed me deeply, and something shifted within me. It was my greatest experience at that workshop and the most personally moving Family Reconstruction I've ever done.

When we ended, it was around 3 o'clock in the morning. A man in a wheelchair stayed behind. He had steel-blue eyes that I'll never forget. "Can I wheel you back to your room?" I asked.

"I have to talk to you first." He had not played a role. Because of his wheelchair, the star had invited him to be an observer. Now he felt he had to tell me that, when he was six or seven years old, he'd had to go to a Hitler Youth Camp. Later, he had joined the SS. "After watching this Family Reconstruction, I really don't think I can live with myself," he told me. "I am so terribly ashamed that I was part of all that."

I had once vowed that if I ever had the chance to look into the eyes of an SS officer, I would spit. The SS was the worst organization, the Nazi elite. They had the greatest power for killing. Now was my chance.

I couldn't do it, of course. A huge shift had already taken place. Looking into his eyes, I said, "I want you to live. There is nothing you could do about what happened to you. You were swept up into the system." For me, these words were a revelation that came as I was speaking. They just tumbled out of my mouth and into his eyes. In the long talk that followed, I was begging him to choose to live. "I can't believe what I'm doing," I told him. "I don't believe this is happening to me." I felt such compassion for him that it surprised me. I felt myself letting go of my hatred, the burden of resentment I had carried for so long.

On the last day of the workshop, I told the whole group that I hadn't wanted to come, that I hadn't wanted to be there, because I couldn't believe there would be a single true human being among them. In response, many of the people in the group told me they had been just as afraid. They knew I was from Hungary originally and had lived through the war. They knew how I might feel about them, and they all had that chip on their shoulders. No one had expressed this before, of course. They were simply on guard.

True, these people didn't reflect all of Germany—the workshop was for select professionals—but for me, they reflected the possibilities. Then and there, I decided that I would never again be judgmental. I'd never forgive or forget the Nazi years, but judgment belongs to the Nuhrenberg trials and to a higher level beyond me, in which I do believe.

I'd gotten in touch with the humanity of these people. As usual, Paul had been right. For my first forty-nine years, I had seen and judged people as being good or bad, right or wrong. I did not think in terms of process. I later realized that the story was not important, but the underlying process was.

I also learned from how Virginia was teaching me during this time. She was not telling me what to do but just giving me some directions and allowing me to proceed in my own way. She gave me the freedom to learn, saying, "You will make a mistake. People will survive. These people have survived much more than your mistake." That experience set the foundation to do what I'm doing today. And I now know that I'm doing it well.

Shortly before this, on June 7, 1979, my grandson Steve was born. It was exactly twenty-five years after my father's death, which made we wonder. Steve was a beautiful baby, and Paul and I were delighted to have a second grandchild.

—·•·—

Three months later, on September 21, Paul said, "I want the family here for dinner tonight." This seemed somewhat unusual to me, as we saw them often, but I phoned Andy. He said they could come the next evening. We had a nice time, and for the first time, Paul talked about his family, his ancestors and relatives. Carol drew a family map for him.

Little Paul stayed with us that night, and the next day was a beautiful day. "Papa Paul" and Paul had a wonderful day playing together. Papa found a huge box and Paul crawled in and out. They had great fun.

After we took our grandson home, Paul and I had dinner and a lovely evening together. As usual, he turned on the television around 11 o'clock to hear the news. I noticed how hard he was breathing. I thought he was having an asthma attack. When he gasped, "Phone," I ran to the kitchen and called for an ambu-

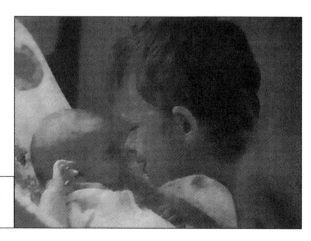

Steve and Paul
1979

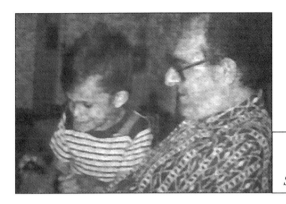

*Paul with his
grandfather
September 23, 1979*

lance. It was the last word he said. By the time I got back, he had fallen off his chair. I knew he was dead but didn't believe it. It was September 23, 1979.

I phoned Andy, hoping he could rush the ambulance. Then I tried everything I knew to revive Paul: mouth-to-mouth resuscitation, talking to him. When nothing worked, I went completely crazy. I just couldn't believe what was happening. It was the biggest shock in my life, and it was all so sudden. I couldn't even tell him goodbye. I wanted to die. I just did not want to have that pain. Losing Paul was worse than anything I had ever experienced.

Andy ran over, and the ambulance arrived. At the nearby Misericordia Hospital, doctors tried everything to revive Paul. Nothing worked. His brain had stopped working. At 3 A.M., they pronounced him dead.

After Paul's open-heart surgery in mid 1974, the cardiologist had suggested that Paul would live another five years, the standard prognosis at the time. We hadn't taken that seriously, given Paul's restored health. When he really did die in September 1979, it was a shock to us all.

I couldn't go home. Instead, I went to Andy's house. The next morning found me still sitting in the den, crying. Around 7 o'clock, Andy plunked little Paul down in a chair and said, "You tell him." Andy didn't know how to break the news. Paul, who was four and a half, knew that something very unusual was going on, if I was at their house early in the morning and crying.

I told Paul, "I have to tell you something very sad. Papa died." This was his first encounter with death.

"Where is Papa now?" Paul asked.

"He is still in the hospital, but he will be put in a place called a morgue," I said.

"I have to talk to him, because I am Superman. We've played this game very often. Papa dies and I say, 'Get up,' and he gets up. The same when I die."

"No, this is not a game," I told him. I tried to explain that Paul would never come back again. Thinking and thinking, little Paul sort of took it in. Then I said, "I will miss him, because I will be alone now, Paul, for the rest of my life."

Again, he thought very hard. Then he said, "Babi, you will never be alone. I will be with you, and my daddy will be with you, and when I die, Steve will be with you." In his mind, I would survive everyone.

"I know you will be with me, but I will really miss Papa." I just had to have this talk. He was only a small child, but he was the only person I could really talk to then. In their grief, the others didn't want to talk about it.

He said, "You know, Babi, Papa is with us right now, and he will be everywhere and he will help us, take care of us, because he is around. I know it."

"Can you see him?" I asked.

"No, stupid, I feel it. And he will be here always."

The next day, he insisted on going to the funeral home. First, he wanted to write his grandfather a letter. He couldn't write yet, of course, so he scribbled on a big piece of paper. "Only Papa can read this," he said. Then we went to the funeral home, where he looked at Paul and said, "Papa, that's enough now. You've been here since yesterday. You get up now." He tried all the tricks they'd played.

"Touch his hand," I told him, "He's cold. This is being dead."

When nothing happened, he said to Paul, "I wrote you a letter, and I want to put it on you because only you can read it." His sense of connection with Paul was so strong that, for years after that, whenever he wanted something, he would say, "Papa, help us." Or, when anyone remarked on how well he did in school, he'd reply, "It's easy, because Papa is helping me." if we drove somewhere, I'd hear him say, "Papa, help us to find parking." Then, when I found a parking spot, he'd tell me, "You see, Papa helps us."

Andy and I wanted the funeral to be a celebration of Paul's beliefs and his life. This fit with what Paul wanted, we knew from the letter he'd written to Andy before the open-heart surgery. In my heart, I would have liked for him to have a Jewish funeral. However, Andy and I decided to be congruent with the original decision that Paul and I had made to keep our Jewish

*Me with Andy
after Paul's death
1979*

background private. We chose to hold a totally nondenominational service.

Paul had always said he wanted Joan Herrick to do his funeral. A close friend and therapist from Palo Alto, California, she was also qualified to conduct funerals. I phoned to ask her and, after she got over the shock of Paul's death, Joan called back and said yes. She would come to Winnipeg for the funeral on Wednesday, September 26.

Paul loved music, so a friend of his set up a sound system in the funeral home. We played his two favorite pieces: Mahler's "Fourth Symphony" and "The Sting." The Mahler piece represented Paul's serious and tragic part; "The Sting" was his fun-loving part. Paul had been on the board of the Winnipeg symphony, and for years he had fought to put Mahler on the program. His oldest friend in Winnipeg, George Lockwood, told me later that it was the perfect choice for his funeral. He said Paul had told him once that he didn't want to die until Winnipeg had heard Mahler.

Paul loved people, and we had asked various people to speak at the funeral about different aspects of his life. These included a friend who talked about his commitment to Rotary, a friend from our Hungarian group, and others. Virginia spoke on behalf of the IHLRN group. She began by talking about how Paul would cut her toenails. Nobody understood why Virginia Satir would talk about this, but it was a very intimate aspect of their relationship. She had very big toes and strong nails, and Paul was the only person she trusted to clip her toenails. He was used to clipping toenails on dogs. Then she said, "Some people seek to have monuments, but Paul had only one monument: his humanness and his love for people. He loved animals, and he loved women. That is the most important monument for his life. He left all these loving messages." In the middle of a sentence, she started to cry and went back to her seat. Later, she told me, "Paul gave me a gift through his death. I have never before cried in front of a group of people, and I just couldn't keep from crying." Meanwhile, we asked people to take flowers from his casket, to represent Paul's sharing and giving.

———•◦•••◦•———

A few weeks after the funeral, Virginia was headed for the IHLRN meeting in Mexico. "Give me a tape of the funeral so I can have a memorial for Paul with the IHLRN group. Everybody in the group loved him, and it's in a place that he loved."

Andy responded, "Well, if there's going to be a memorial for Paul, then we want to be there." Earlier, I had canceled my plans to attend the conference. Now it seemed like a good idea to go. A few weeks later, we went back to that beautiful spot where Paul had spent so many great times with Virginia.

The service was held in a beautifully renovated old carriage room that overlooked part of the garden, and all the doors were open. On a long table covered with a hundred roses, we replayed the music and the whole funeral. People had a chance to share their feelings and their memories about Paul. I felt as though he was there, especially when the leaves of one tree fell down all at once.

It took me a very long time to come back to life after Paul's death. I experienced the loss like never before. The pain, the bitterness, the despair, the anger, the end of a thirty-seven-year relationship—they whirled around, over and over. The pain was too much to live with. Often, I was trying to think of painless ways to die. I missed Paul. By the end of our living together for over three decades, we had achieved an intimacy that was no longer enmeshed but loving and free.

*Paul's memorial
1979*

I missed his loving and our partnership. Most of all, I felt deeply sad that he who enjoyed living so much was no longer here. For a long time, I did not accept his dying. I did not want sympathy from others. I thought that I should have died instead. Many people told me the usual things: it will take time, you're strong, it'll be okay, and so on. This just left me feeling alone, angry, and not understood.

In this most difficult period, Ben and Jock helped me the most to survive my biggest crisis. Nothing made any sense any more. I felt that they understood my grief and my loss in the deepest sense. That helped me feel less alone in the world. When I was thinking about suicide, Ben told me that whatever I decided, they would support and understand me. That gave me permission to live as well as to die.

Paul had connected wonderfully with Ben and Jock, and they did with him. After his death, they named a dining room after him in their Gabriola Island lodge (where they hold their PD seminars). Called the Gomori Room, it features our pictures.

Another friend, Bob Spitzer, said, "Just wait six months, and then we'll talk again." He, too, said he would understand if I could not.

My friend Eleanor, who also had known Paul, was a special support for me in Winnipeg. As another Eleanor once wrote, "It is a curious thing in human experience, but to live through a period of stress and sorrow with another person creates a bond which nothing seems able to break."*

Andy had his own grief, and he tried to take care of me as well. However, I didn't want to establish a relationship in which he became my caretaker and I became his burden. Nor did I want to be a widow who can't stand on her own feet. All the same, I soon realized how spoiled I was. Paul had done many things around our home without a word. For example, soon after he died, a light went out in the kitchen. I phoned Andy to send me an electrician, telling him something was wrong with my electricity. Andy came over, looked at the light, and changed the bulb. I did not know about such things because Paul did all that.

What kept me alive were Andy and his children, Paul and Steve. Steve was only three months old when Paul died, unfortunately, so he never had a chance to experience his grandfather. When they visited me together, little Paul showed Steve all the

Paul and Steve
1981

---

* Eleanor Roosevelt (1996), p. 32.

games that Paul had played with him, so that Steve would get a feel for his grandfather. We played, and we danced to "The Sting."

Later, around the age of five and a half, Paul would come over and tell me to put on "Papa's music." This went back to the days when I went away to a workshop, and the two of them would visit on their own. Sitting together, they would listen to Mahler. So now I would put on a record, and little Paul would walk around in the room, listening. When I asked what he was doing, he said, "I am with Papa, through his music."

I always fed them something, but it wasn't the typical grandmother kind of things. I never baked anything or cooked special meals. They chose what they liked and wanted, and we often went out to eat. "You are an unusual grandmother," Steve said when he was little. They also often came to the airport when I left or came home, so when he was three or four years old, he told some people, "I have a grandmother who lives in an airplane." Steve was his own person from the beginning. He was stubborn, and for three years he was very selective about food. I worried that he wouldn't grow, and sometimes I smuggled an egg into his chocolate milk. He'd notice and refuse to drink it. Eventually, he did add a few more foods—such as chicken, fries, and pizza— but he never touched vegetables. Then again, neither do I.

Steve did grow. Today, he's taller than Paul and Andy. He's in his twenties now and is following his dream of becoming an actor. He believes in himself, he is a free spirit, and I hope he'll get what he wants. I don't see him often enough, as he currently lives in Vancouver. I feel close to him and we are friends. Steve is a beautiful person. Even though he chose a difficult and challenging path, he goes for it with consistency. I respect his knowing what he wants and his commitment to pursuing it.

I enjoyed watching Paul and Steve grow up and being able to be part of their lives. My greatest joy was to take them to movies and the theater and tell them stories. We went to plays, we danced, and we did all kinds of things together. We are connected.

By then, I knew more about children than when Andy was a child. I also learned a lot from my grandsons. Paul used to say, "What keeps grandparents and grandchildren close is that they both criticize the parents." This was sometimes true for me, too.

Over time, I took on more work at St. Boniface. For awhile, however, whenever a couple came in and presented their problems, I would think, "How come this is a problem? You're both alive. Close your eyes and just imagine that the other one is dead." That was the extent of my technique, given my state of mind. So I decided not to see couples for the time being. I cut back on certain kinds of work and did more workshops instead.

After Paul's death, I also began distancing myself from our couple friends. I suddenly felt that I was not fitting in. I did not pity myself, but I was miserable company. I decided to be straight about how I felt, to myself and to others. I handled my frustration and all my feelings by expressing them. I did not want them swelling and boiling inside me, which I believe leads to dying from cancer. Even when people asked the usual rhetorical question, "How are you?" I'd say, "I feel awful, I want to die." They stopped asking.

It took me about three and a half years before I consciously decided that I wanted to be healthy and keep living. What really helped me was Ben and Jock's idea that I can have Paul in my heart always, that he is with me. It's not that the sun shouldn't shine because he is not here. At first sight, Paul had said our marriage was written in heaven. I did not believe it then, but he convinced me. And he was right. Despite his death in 1979, I know we're connected as if we were still married.

I believe that we are here to learn, so I had to make sense out of Paul's untimely death. I realized that I had never lived alone—and I was never as alone as I was during this time of grief. Learning to live by myself was difficult. I still don't like it, so I wouldn't say I got used to it. However, I did get through it, making my own decisions and being totally free from anybody else. Nobody was telling me what to do or what not to do.

At the same time, I was making my own mistakes, too. Most of the time, I do only what I want to do. I won't do anything I don't want to do. In a way, this "I won't" attitude is becoming a life style. It keeps me healthy, although I break all the rules of healthy living. I sleep five hours because more is a waste of time. I eat little and only what I like, not the "right" things, such as vegetables or vitamins. My life is not boring, and I could not live any other way.

I no longer take on any work that I don't want to do. For example, I don't take assignments like talking to a group of people for an hour over lunch or dinner. I also won't be with people I don't want to be with, which seems like a waste of time. I don't break commitments, but I take the time to decide whether I want to do something before I make a commitment. I'm still doing a lot of things that come from the past, such as placating people. I have a very hard time saying no. I had to learn how. I need to tell myself, "I won't," too.

When I realized that making my own decisions and learning to live on my own were two of my tasks for this life, it was easier to go ahead. This was how I eventually got to a point where I could decide what I wanted to do with the rest of my life.

Growth and learning can come from any situation or experience, problem or crisis.

—*Virginia Satir*

Only if outward and inner freedom are constantly and consciously pursued is there a possibility of spiritual development and perfection and thus of improving man's outward and inner life.

—*Albert Einstein*

— *14* —

Transformations

After Paul's death, I spent more and more time at Satir workshops. A slow learner, I worked with Virginia for about nineteen years, during which I listened and made tons of notes. I learned her tools and used them in a creative way, with freedom and excitement. I was and I am excited and attracted to living and working in this way. Because she was often in Winnipeg and people at the hospital knew her, they supported my requests to leave for a month-long workshop now and then. Getting time off was not a problem, because I always came back with new ideas.

I continued learning to use myself in a more congruent way. This included sharing my own feelings or experiences with clients, when appropriate. This was contrary to what I had learned in the School of Social Work. I believe in the use of the self—that is, relating through my own experiences and my own feelings in addition to what I've learned.

My experience and my belief are that congruence leads to mental and physical health. Being straight with people—and with myself—is one of my greatest values. People know they can trust me to say what is true for me. There's no game playing in it. Congruence also leads to harmony within the self, the family, and the world. As Virginia said, the family is a microcosm of the world. Put together the existing families, and we have community and society. To understand the world, we need to understand the family. The issues are the same: power, autonomy, intimacy, trust, communication, and more. All these underlie how we live in the world.

I also learned more about paying attention to process rather than content. This was easy for me. My whole life had been a process of evolving experiences, often out of my control. However, it took me a long time to feel competent with the process of Virginia's work. One day, after many years of working together, she asked, "How are the families you are working with doing?"

"Families?! I can't work with families yet. I don't know enough." I had always wanted to use and teach what I was learning, but the idea of plunging into a session with the entire family still scared me.

"Let me show you how to begin working with families." I thought she was about to give me her great magic wisdom. Instead, she took my hand and asked me to stand. Then we took one step together, then another, and one more. Then we stopped. "If we fall down into a ditch," she explained, "we'll crawl right back out and go on. That's how you start to work with families."

"I might fail," I warned.

"You will learn from your failures."

I did, and I do. When I got back to Winnipeg, I made an appointment with the family of a patient who was on the psychiatric ward. It would be my first family interview. On our way to meet with them, my patient stopped for a moment and said, "I am so scared."

"I'm scared, too," I told her. "Let's be scared together."

That first family interview worked. Again, it was not because of my vast experience but because I knew the process. So I had risked starting, and the process had worked. It is the process that works, and I gradually learned to trust that.

This reminds me of another significant influence in my life. Over the last twenty years, I have been fortunate to meet and learn from many excellent people, all of whom affected my personal and professional development. One of these was Carl Whitaker, who broke many of the rules of therapy as he worked toward authentic experiences with each family. Professional Education, Inc. often brought him to Winnipeg, and I went to many of his workshops. He would interview a family and then hold amazingly open discussions with the audience, giving us direct answers to our questions.

Many of his statements stayed with me long after the workshops because his views were so fresh and individual. He believed that each human experience—and the essence of each person, whether therapist or client—is unique. We take away from that and move away from each other if we make generalizations or talk on a theoretical level. We lose touch with the essence of others and ourselves.

To respond to uniqueness, the therapist needs to be authentic. So Carl did not talk about theories or use dry, logical processes much. He knew all the theories, but he was true to himself when in action. He wanted to help other therapists give themselves permission to do the same thing: to stay with their clients on the authentic level of experience.

Sometimes his humanness was surprising. For example, if he suddenly was reminded of a dream he'd had, or if his neck got sore, he would talk about it wilth the family. He said this gave clients permission to share their own physical or personal experiences, which might break through to a deeper, more authentic level.

Carl was always teasing people. He had a great sense of humor and challenged people through the ridiculous. For example, at one of his Winnipeg presentations, he worked with a family with a long-term alcohol problem. After the interview, he shook hands with everybody and told the mother that she would continue to drink and that she should find a bartender for a boyfriend. She got very angry and told him she felt as though she were on the television program Candid Camera. Then, a few weeks later, she told her regular therapist, "Tell that son of a bitch that I gave up drinking. He was wrong!"

So, instead of being confined to one theory or school of thought, he was just Whitaker—in all his uniqueness. For me, his existential experiential family therapy fit very well with Virginia's perspectives and my own. Carl worked very much on the unconscious, spontaneous level. He thought his dreams often had something to do with his sessions, even if he didn't yet know what the connection might be. He'd offer his dreams, trusting that the client would make a connection of benefit. So I learned that whatever happens to me has something to do with what's happening to the people in front of me.

I also learned a lot about therapeutic boundaries and ethical considerations. Carl was one of the most honest and ethical people I knew. He also had very strong boundaries. For example, I learned that it was okay to share about myself and my own life but not to share other people's stories without their permission. I'm very careful about that now. In sharing my own experiences, I also learned to stick to issues that I've already resolved, because posing my current, unresolved issues is a way of asking the client to assume the role of therapist.

Carl's use of self encouraged me to feel freer to be myself. He was also very daring, which helped me learn to do and say things more spontaneously. Sometimes, after he said the most outrageous things in a session, people in the audience asked, "Why did you say that?"

"Well, you know, maybe it made sense and maybe it didn't," he'd reply, "but that is where I was. This is what came to me." To me, what he said was always relevant. Again, that helped me to be freer. To me, it meant that wherever I am may relate to where other people are.

I'm not sure the work of Carl Whitaker can be learned through any formal process. Parts of what he modeled and taught did release others to approach therapy differently. Some people can do this more than others. I could never come close to his outrageous daring, but I did learn to be more open and adventurous, to use my sense of humor, to be me, and to challenge people.

Meanwhile, in the late 1970s, a lot of my energy was going to events connected with Virginia's Avanta network. She had founded Avanta in 1976 with the main purpose of training people from all over the world to teach her work and to continue sharing. For eight years, from 1981 to 1988, she led a month-long training workshop every summer. The first was in 1981 in Utah, where I was a trainer for the first time. The next year, Virginia's summer training moved permanently to Colorado.

Ninety people from various countries participated. The trainees worked in triads, or threesomes, to conduct the afternoon groups of thirty participants each. While Virginia taught the introductory ("Level 1") group, my triad—Jane Gerber, John Banmen, and I—developed and taught the advanced training module ("Level 2"). Our triad continued this until 1989.

The annual training in Colorado gave Avanta members the opportunity to connect with people with whom Virginia had a teaching relationship all over the world. Once, when she was sick, Virginia sent me to Venezuela to do a workshop in her place. Afraid that the participants would be disappointed, I insisted that the organizers phone them ahead of time to say that they weren't getting Virginia. Almost everybody came anyway.

After I began doing workshops with Virginia, people sometimes invited my triad to give workshops. At times, Virginia also sent someone from Avanta to do work on his or her own. So, especially after Paul's death in 1979, I increased my involvement with teaching and traveling. My home became a place where I changed my luggage and looked after my mail. I live in the midst of chaos. Paul used to say that if chaos does not come to me, I create it. I think this is true. I am never up to date with

Virginia with her Crested Butte staff, 1982
(standing, left to right:) Bill Kelly, Ken Block, Joe Dillen, John Banmen;
(sitting, left to right:) me, Michele Baldwin, Virginia, Jane Gerber,
Alla Destandau, and Meryl Tullis

the everyday tasks. My filing system is a mess, and I sometimes spend hours looking for things. Time is important for me, yet I have difficulty delegating mundane tasks and do everything myself. Despite this, I am always on time and somehow get where I need to be. I have high energy and can work twelve hours a day when I am with people. I believe that my work provides me with energy. It's a two-way exchange, in my experience. It is a surprise whenever I feel tired. Usually, it's related to agreeing to something that I did not want to do.

Jane, John, and I led many workshops in South America and Asia. Virginia's model travels well because it deals with universal human processes. Because these exist everywhere, the Satir model applies to all cultures of human beings. Feelings are the same worldwide, no matter people's color, age, or race.

In 1983, our triad was invited to do a workshop in Hong Kong. That led to invitations from people in Taiwan, which led to invitations from others in Thailand. For fifteen years since then, I have returned every year to do one or more workshops. In the last few years, I have gone to Hong Kong and Taiwan twice a

*Our triad:
me, John Banmen,
and Jane Gerber
1987*

year and have ongoing teaching responsibilities there. Recently, I started work in Singapore as well. I feel reassured, knowing that my students teach and work with the Satir model at various levels in their countries. Recently, this has included China.

I was very fortunate to meet my friend Marie Lam in Hong Kong. She has been my translator since 1986. I could not teach without her. The quality of her work is outstanding. She not only translates but experiences the process and conveys it with feeling and soul. She knows my work, and we are a team.

Marie is also a great example of change and transformation. Once a traditional Chinese housewife and mother of five, she had a passion to learn and to grow. With courage and consistency, she took the risk of changing. Today, she is a professional woman who has raised her children and now does her own work in Hong Kong and Taiwan.

With each new trip to Asia, I got more in touch with how much Buddhism and eastern philosophy fit me. I find the culture fascinating. The values are very beautiful, and people's spirituality is real and profound. I love the people I have met in Asia. They are curious, hard working, and loving. As I am there every six months, I have developed friendships and feel very close to many. I enjoy experiencing the steady changes they make in their lives as time goes on. Many of the women are interested in being more authentic and autonomous, and some have made great transformations in their personal and professional lives. The Satir model fits their beliefs. They are curious to learn about themselves and to discover that they can enrich their own lives while staying close and connected to their families. It is a privilege to be invited to teach them and to play with them.

I also love connecting people, as mentioned, so I recommended various Personal Development (PD) seminars to my friends in Asia. Many went and participated. Recognizing the value of Ben and Jock's teachings, they invited them to Asia. So Ben and Jock started coming to Hong Kong and Taiwan, too. In addition, a group of students from Taiwan now goes to Gabriola each summer for a two-week seminar.

John Banmen, Jane Gerber, and I were instrumental in founding the Satir centers in Hong Kong, Taiwan, and other places. With Virginia, we also wrote *The Satir Model*, which came out in 1991. The American Association for Marriage and Family Therapy gave this book its Research and Education Award in 1994. This book was also translated into Mandarin.

Meanwhile, I grew very interested in working with families. In 1981, I started a private practice and resigned from the Department of Social Work at St. Boniface Hospital. By then, the administration of hospitals had become so oriented to the bottom line that all my efforts went into preserving the financial status quo. I wasn't keen on spending my time in budget meetings and fighting for my department's share of the money.

For fourteen years as the head of that department, I had wonderful people to work with and I enjoyed my job. When I left my position, the system had recognized and integrated our department's staff of twenty-seven social workers. They were already well trained in family therapy, and now I wanted to teach family therapy in the community.

The hospital administrator asked, "Why would you do it somewhere else? Do it here, in the hospital."

My idea was to teach and to attract people from outside the hospital, so I told him I wanted to work in a neutral place, such as the Outpatient Department. Family therapy is related to every aspect of health, not only to psychiatry, and I wanted to demonstrate that. He agreed, and I became a floating member of the staff. I wouldn't accept being paid out of funds for my former department, saying, "If you want me to stay here, you have to find other money." That never happened, but general practitioners in the hospital lent me their office and referred families to me.

I believe that, no matter what form it takes, the family unit is what links us to society as a whole. To change the family is to change the world. To change the world is to change the family. Why? Everyone who holds power or a position in the world was once a child. How he or she uses power now was learned in the family. Who he or she is as a person was learned in the family. As Virginia wrote,

> Your birth, my birth, everyone's birth is a spiritual event and a cause of celebration . . . we need to provide the richest context possible so that each child can grow up to be fully human.*

Teaching troubled families to become nurturing increases each member's humanity and then spreads into institutions, schools, and government. The family can thus be involved in creating a more fully human world.

Eventually, the new head of the Department of Psychiatry, who was an ambitious person, suggested, "You want to teach family therapy, and I want to develop a new Department of Psychiatry. I'll give you a room where you can do whatever you need to do, as long as you do it here." In this new space, I developed a training program for psychiatric residents and other health professionals. Building it from nothing interested me immensely, and it worked out fine.

---

* *The New Peoplemaking*, p. 337.

A child psychiatrist who planned to develop an adolescent treatment unit wanted to involve the families of his patients. This gave me the chance both to work with families and to teach the process to other health professionals. The program did not turn the psychiatric residents into specialists in family therapy, but it got them to recognize that there's a family behind everyone. Eventually, this became a disciplinary program in psychiatry at the Faculty of Medicine. Psychiatric residents participated for six months or a year. We also included professional participants from social work, nursing, and psychology.

Around this time, I met Eleanor Adaskin, who later became my closest friend in Winnipeg. Her nursing specialty was in family therapy, and she was interested and supportive in developing the training program. We had a working relationship on many fronts. She knew Paul, and we have since spent many fun times going to movies, laughing, and loving to be together. We've worked together for many years since then, and I enjoy writing with her. She translates my thoughts from my Hungarian English into her beautiful English language.

Me with Eleanor
1973

When I lead a workshop, I know where I am going. I appreciate every person as a unique challenge and recognize the opportunity for assisting in his or her constructive transformation. I don't plan how to get there. I just go step by step wherever the participants are going, following the process and sensing what fits. In workshops, everybody needs something different, so I bring a lot of things I've learned and use them in a flexible way. Inspired by Ben and Jock, respectively, I incorporate music and poetry in my work. In this way, my own method of thinking and feeling helps me challenge others to do something constructive for themselves. I really believe that's what growth and life are about. I believe that we have choices.

My goals are that people will know more about themselves, trust themselves more, have more self-esteem, and feel better about themselves. Everything after that has to do with breaking down the walls and building the bridges for them to get there in relation to other people and, most important, in relation to themselves. I've found that people also learn a lot from and provide support for each other.

In her work, Virginia was very smooth, loving, and nice— sometimes even too nice. From Ben and Jock, I learned to be more challenging, more straight, and more blunt. I combined the beautiful places where she, Ben, Jock, and others were coming from and started expressing myself in a more confronting way. That combination helps me not to be like any of them but to be me.

I do respect wherever each person is, and I also challenge as much as I can. I sense how far each person's system can go and where I need to stop. What often helps is a gift: my intuition. I somehow get a feeling about each person I'm working with, and when I check it out, it proves to be true.

Another thing I bring to my clients and to workshops is my faith in people: that they each can grow and do their own thing. I believe that all human beings have all the resources they need— the same resources I have—so I merely have to provide the opportunity for them to find access to those resources and make their own choices about how to use them. My energy and my belief in each person's strength somehow create a link between us and, in turn, people resonate while empowering themselves. I think that's the biggest gift I can offer. Encouraging people to become aware of what they want, I challenge them to work toward it.

If we are all energy, we have choices about how to use that energy. For example, some people I've met have developed resources for and spend lots of energy on protecting themselves. Maybe this kind of protection was often useful in their growing up, but it is no longer needed or useful in their adult lives. Growing from our experiences is a step toward growth and transformation.

———————

In 1978, Paul and I were fortunate to participate in a five-day workshop with another special teacher and therapist, Dr. Milton Erickson. My friend Joan Winter organized this time with him at his office for fifteen of us from the Avanta group. The office was in a one-room building outside the small house in Phoenix where he and his wife lived.

The room had no furniture, so we all sat on the floor. Estensively paralyzed from polio, Erickson was in a wheelchair. A natural storyteller, he taught by telling stories about his patients. He made only a few direct statements. Whenever we asked a question, he'd respond by saying, "That reminds me of so and so" and telling another story. For instance, Paul told him, "I have a problem because I have a heart condition and I have an asthma condition. When I take a pill for my asthma that is not good for my heart and vice versa. I don't know what to do."

Erickson's response was, "That reminds me of my children. I have eight children, and every Christmas each of my children got a present from me. Sometimes one of them was a very expensive one—a bicycle, say—and the other one would only get a pin." It depended what they needed, he said, but he treated them equally and took care of them equally. "The important thing is that I loved them all. And it was never at the expense of the others." Everything was related to our questions indirectly, so we'd have to put the puzzle together later. In the evenings, some of us got together to figure out why he'd told that day's particular stories. Paul interpreted his answer to mean that he had to treat his lungs and his heart in an equal way, and not to have the negative energy about "this hurts my heart, and this hurts my lungs."

An hour after the first story, Erickson had said, "Now, I'm going to tell a story about a little boy who had asthma. His parents wanted to take care of him and didn't let him to go and play with the other kids. They didn't let him out into the garden, and they didn't let him do anything that little boys want to do. So he became more and more sick because his parents were only looking after his health and not after his quality of life.

"Then they brought him to me. He was five or six years old. I said, 'Just let him be. Let him live. Let him play hockey, and let him do everything. Because even if he dies earlier, at least he will have been living.'"

I know this was a message to me. I was so worried about Paul's health that I constantly told him not to do this and not to do that—not to do anything. He had a lot of restrictions, and he had to do lots of exercises. Sometimes he joked, "You know, I'm going to die because I take so much care of myself."

Erickson continued: "Then the parents got really worried again and started to restrict him. They gave him the medication again. And then this little boy died." That was all he said. Paul and I knew that this was a message to us.

This story disturbed Paul very much, and that night he dreamed about this little boy's funeral. He thought he was dreaming about his own funeral. In the morning, when we met Erickson, Paul said "You know, I had this dream, and I'm concerned now why I had this dream. Does it have a meaning?"

Erickson looked at him. "Paul, there is one thing that is important: it wasn't your funeral. It was that little boy's funeral. It's not yours. Never forget that." And we didn't.

Erickson talked in detail about his experiences with patients. After describing somebody, he would talk about his interventions. He expressed so much love and so much caring for these people that we had tears in our eyes. This was the opposite of what I had expected at first. Before I met him, I had read about his cases in books written about him, and they sounded very manipulative. Now that I heard him tell the same stories in person, what came across were his continued interest, caring, and love for his patients. He was totally devoted to them. Many of them wrote him every Christmas for over twenty years, and he showed us these letters and presents with tremendous love. He had terrific follow-up stories about these former clients. He knew when they got married and had children or grandchildren.

One of Erickson's philosophies struck me especially. "Never belong to one school of thought," he said. "Never stick to one therapeutic approach. Be broad minded and flexible." Becoming myself and trusting myself came gradually for me. First, I'd integrate what I learned from my teachers. Over time, I'd throw away whatever didn't fit. Finally, I always came back to following my intuition.

He told us that we knew more than we thought we knew and that we should give ourselves permission to know all that we knew. I learned more in those five days than I realized at the time. Something happened to me on a subconscious level. Indeed, I had started to trust my intuition, my creativity, and myself. I learned to have faith in myself and in the energy of all people.

In my work with people, I use a lot of Erickson's techniques. I learned to give people tasks so that they could build self-esteem from their own experiences. Erickson's creativity in this area was remarkable.

The combination of Satir and Erickson was a powerful experience and learning to absorb. For a long time, I had tried to think like Virginia. I kept thinking, "What would she do?" That didn't work, so I could not go on like that. Then, after I experienced Erickson, I started to ask, "Well, what would Maria do?" Trusting my own self took a long time. Gradually, I began listening to what my intuition was telling me. That, too, was an important transformation. I was taking my learnings into myself, integrating them, and then trusting myself with the process. That's when I stopped planning ahead and started listening more to people. Over the years, I found this always led me to each next step.

———

By 1991, I realized that my traveling and my private practice no longer left me enough time to teach at St. Boniface. I did not know how I was going to manage without my twenty-six-year-old routine of working in that hospital whenever I was in

Winnipeg. My nature is to be very unstructured, so I worried about losing that organized part of my daily life. I was also very committed to the program, which was my baby.

Fortunately, one of the psychiatrists in our program, with whom I'd worked for two years, was interested in taking charge of it. I left the training program in good hands, with two colleagues and friends. Much to my pleasure, he hired me as a consultant. Once or twice a week, I would go in and watch the teaching from behind a one-way mirror. That felt very good because I didn't have to cut my umbilical cord right away. I could go in as I wanted, and I didn't even notice when I no longer had time to continue. I had phased myself out but not consciously. My private practice and my traveling kept me so busy that I had less and less time. By the time I separated from the program completely, I didn't feel any loss.

At that time, I started the Satir Institute in Winnipeg. For many years, Eleanor Adaskin served as its president. The other large part of my life was taking place at my second home, Gabriola Island. To this day, I love being there and would be there much

*Ben and Jock
1988*

more often, if I had time. Ben and Jock and the other friends I've
made there mean an awful lot to me. I also participate in their PD
seminar programs, which are compatible with Virginia's teaching
and philosophy. I have learned about bioenergetics and the deep
connection between body, mind, and spirit. These learnings
enriched and added a lot to what I already knew. Whenever I
can, I participate in Ben and Jock's programs on East–West
philosophy, Chinese medicine, acupuncture, and beyond. Since
1988, I have taught workshops about the Satir model once a year
on Gabriola.

Creativity and humor are important in my connecting with
people. This was especially true during a particular workshop I
led in Thailand. The participants included a group of monks
whose vows didn't allow talking directly with women or taking
anything directly from them. A translator played the middle person (even though I think they understood English). She told me
that the monks wouldn't do any role-plays because they were
afraid they might trip over their robes. Otherwise, they were very
deferential and had a good sense of humor. The younger ones
would take notes while the older ones just paid attention. They
could tell what I was thinking just by watching.

At lunch and dinner, we sat at tables next to one another.
On the second or third day, I asked my translator to ask the monks
why they couldn't take anything directly from the hands of a
woman. After she translated, the monks looked back and asked
what I thought. In a fun tone of voice, I told the translator, "I
think you're afraid women may seduce you. You are afraid of us.
That is why you cannot touch anything that we touch."

They laughed, and the translator said, "No, that's not it."
They never did tell me why, but it was fascinating to me.

At the end of the workshop, one of the old monks spoke to the group. The translator told me, "You just got the biggest compliment a monk can give." The old man had said I was a good teacher in spite of being a woman. That was the compliment.

He went on to compliment Virginia, too. The monks felt that the underlying philosophy they learned at the workshop matched their philosophy. (I don't generally discuss philosophy or beliefs in my workshops, I simply integrate them in my work.) The monk wanted to know if Virginia was Buddhist. I was not surprised, because I knew that Virginia's spirituality reflected the beliefs of the world's great spiritual leaders. I told him that she knew about Buddhism, and she had her own philosophy.

Love, hope, meaning, and the beauty of the human spirit were central to Virginia's beliefs and to her process of transformative work. She was a visionary, a spiritual leader. In speaking unapologetically of hope, love, the "shining light of the spirit," and the "magnificence of the human being," her statements came closer to the spiritual realm than the scientific one. "Recognizing the power of spirit is what healing, living, and spirituality is all about," she said.

Breaking all the rules by mixing therapy with spirituality, she said: "The most lasting spiritual, psychological change occurs when spiritual healing also occurs." I believe that. Virginia also wrote:

> The first step in any change is to contact the spirit. Then, together, we can clear the way to release the energy for going toward health. This, too, is spirituality in action.*

---

* *The New Peoplemaking*, p. 341.

To her, it was also of fundamental importance to establish a relationship with what she called the life force. She believed that we all come into this world with an individual life force and all the resources we need to grow. "How we apply our spiritual essence shows how we value life," she wrote. "I believe that successful living depends on our making and accepting a relationship to our life force." She wrote about growing up on a farm:

> Very early, I understood that growth was life force revealing itself, a manifestation of spirit. . . . Those wondrous feelings remain with me today, and I think they have guided me in finding ways to help people grow.*

All human beings were sacred to Virginia, and capable of change and growth. Growing up and the process of becoming more adult is a process of transformation because it means letting go at every step and taking in the new. Human beings are manifestations of the Universal Energy, she believed, and they can fulfill what they were meant to fulfill. They can use themselves differently, more effectively, and with more choices. Virginia had a deep faith in human beings and their ability to manage their lives from a sense of strength, inner motivation, and personal responsibility. Instinctively, deep down, I already knew all this. However, I needed to bring these ideas into my awareness and put them into action for myself and for others. Doing this changed the purpose and direction of my life.

---

* *The New Peoplemaking*, p. 334.

Of all the means which
wisdom uses to ensure
happiness throughout the
whole of life, by far the most
important is acquisition of
friends.

—*Epicurus*

We either make ourselves
miserable, or we make
ourselves strong, The
amount of work is the same.

—*Carlos Castañeda*

Your work is to discover
your work and then with all
your heart to give yourself
to it.

—*The Buddha*

— *15* —

Epilogue

Revisiting my eighty-odd years of living, I can now appreciate every experience I've had. Virginia grew up on a farm, so she knew all about compost, a substance that starts out seeming unpleasant but later cause things to grow. She used to call such transformation "turning shit into gold."

Each "knot" that developed while growing up served as a challenge later in my life. My search for freedom, learning, and knowledge was rooted in my childhood. Living in four entirely different political systems provided me with a broad perspective and a deep sense of humility. My miraculous escapes and survivals shaped my faith that somehow I was meant to live, as well as giving me an absolute belief in a higher spiritual existence. The opportunities I've had to meet and learn from great teachers have been immense gifts for growth and in my search for purpose.

I learned and still believe that my painful experiences provided me with an opportunity for new discoveries in the world and in myself. Again, I know now that the past doesn't have to contaminate the present. I have the choice to use the past as a learning tool to illuminate the present. I believe this unconditionally, and it is the fundamental premise of my work with people. I have a passion to share these learnings because I am convinced that this self-inflicted contamination by the past leads to many illnesses, both mental and physical.

A great example of this concept is the life and work of Viktor Frankl. He wrote:

> If there is a meaning in life at all, then there must be a meaning in suffering. Suffering is an ineradicable part of life, even as fate and death. . . . without suffering and death, human life cannot be complete. The way in which a man accepts his fate and all the suffering it entails—even under the most difficult circumstances—adds a deeper meaning to his life. Here lies the chance for a man either to make use of or forego the opportunities of attaining the moral values that a difficult situation may afford him.*

Transformation is not a simple process, of course. In my work, I meet many people who use their past experiences to victimize themselves. In all authenticity, I suggest that it is their choice. The "poor me" victim role has its benefits, including the privilege of being irresponsible. Giving up that role has consequences, mainly to do with being responsible for oneself and one's choices.

I believe in personal responsibility. I admire Dr. Thomas Szasz, a fellow Hungarian friend and colleague, for his consistent courage and honesty in challenging the establishment with his ideas for liberty, social responsibility, and people's right to make their own decisions and live with the consequences. His lifelong struggle for justice inspires me to stand up for my own ideas and for myself.

Humor and its essence are important resources in my life and work. Virginia used to say that we are "cosmic jokes," after all, and therefore not to take ourselves too seriously. Ben and Jock laughingly say, "We are all bozos." I do believe that laugh-

* *Man's Search for Meaning*, p. 88.

ing at ourselves is a healing process. For example, half the participants at one workshop introduced themselves as the victims of various experiences. Suggesting a contest, I offered prizes for the three most self-victimized people, to be awarded at the end of the workshop. No one ever claimed these prizes. I felt heard. They had learned self-compassion and appreciated their strength and themselves.

Curiosity is another one of my most cherished resources. It helps me search for the people from whom I can learn. I am constantly yearning to learn more and find new ways to use myself. In essence, this is what keeps me going. The more I learn, to paraphrase the saying, the more I know how much more there is to learn. I still don't know myself fully. My curiosity also gets me beyond feeling desperate or depressed. Instead, I try to find the meaning and the learning from the experience.

I have made many important choices throughout my life. Those choices reflect my faith and values. I believe I made the most important ones with the help of my spirit guides, my guardian angels, who have been with me throughout my life. Many times, they also guided me away from dying as I lived through the war, the death march, the car accident, and many other life-threatening events.

Returning to Hungary during the war from my new life in Paris was not my first choice, and I had felt betrayed, angry, and helpless at the time. Looking back now, however, I have no regrets. To meet Paul and have Andy (and, later, my grandchildren), I would do it again. In addition, I feel enriched by all the experiences that followed. My choice to return was guided by my love for my father, which gave me an important learning: to follow my feelings and my intuition.

The choice to leave my country was probably the most risky one I've ever made, and I am grateful it worked out. The happiest day in my life was when I reached Vienna and knew that Paul and Andy were alive. The hardest day of my life was when Paul died, and the hardest choice was deciding to go on with my life after his death.

Over my lifetime, I had many "knots" and lots of unfinished business. I realize now that peace needs to start within myself. Only then can peace within myself lead to peace with others. My experience in the 1979 workshop in Germany was a huge step in resolving some of my issues with the past. I learned about acceptance, compassion, and humanness. I don't believe in forgiveness, and I am learning to accept that certain things have happened, even if I can't reach the state of forgiveness.

I also struggled with my relationship with my mother. After I made peace with her, I found a new opportunity to open myself to lasting and enriching friendships with women. Virginia was an important awakening experience in my perception of women. From my friend Eleanor, a treasure of a human being, I have learned much about acceptance and loving. With my friend Linda

Linda and me
2000

*Me with Eva
1999*

Nicholls, I feel connected in many ways. We have resonating interests, and we work, travel, and play together. I cherish our friendship, even though it's a long-distance one. And then there is Eva, my friend for over sixty years (with whom I escaped the death march). Our relationship is growing constantly, in spite of living far from each other. As I let go of my prejudices and opened the door, these women—as well as others—came into my life. I am eternally grateful for all of them.

Another huge knot was my relationship with Hungary. I didn't plan it, but the opportunity to untie it simply came along, step by step. One step had to do with the International Family Therapy Association. Based in Europe, it meets in a different country every year. The first meeting was in Prague. At another conference in Amsterdam, in 1993, I presented a paper on Family Reconstruction. Later I attended the meeting that was in Budapest, where I presented two workshops on Satir. This was a very important experience that went beyond my expectations.

In Budapest, I found out that the whole conference—of about a thousand people from Europe and the States—was being held in what was previously known as the Marx–Engels University, where I got my first degree (in economics). On the opening evening, I went up the same steps I had resented climbing for four years after I returned from Paris. Then I heard Hungarian gypsy music. Deeply moved, I started to cry. "I'm at my old university," I thought, "and thank God I'm coming here to teach Satir." That night's opening speaker was the well-known author and family therapist Ivan Boszormenyi-Nagy, so the whole atmosphere became very Hungarian and emotional.

I led both my workshops in English with a psychiatrist translating into Hungarian. I found this very funny. I don't even know the Hungarian words for some of the concepts I learned in English. Hungarian doesn't have words for self-esteem or congruence. My translator knew how to talk around these kinds of words because she had already participated in workshops in Colorado. (This was when I learned that Virginia's book *Peoplemaking* had been translated into Hungarian years before.)

During the introduction, I heard myself say, "I'm a Canadian who was born in Hungary." It was the first time in my life I had said that, although Paul and I had become citizens five years after we got to Canada. I used to tell people that I was born in Hungary and now lived in Canada. It was ironic that, on Hungarian soil in an international organization, I now spontaneously declared this from deep within me. I continued: "This is the first time that I really feel Canadian, and I'm very happy to speak in English and to bring to you what I've learned while I was away." After more than thirty years, I had to go home to my alma mater to integrate the feeling of being Canadian.

For years, I had been afraid to go back to Hungary. Having been in a government position and having left the country illegally, I did not feel safe about crossing that border again. Paul had always wanted to go back to visit, and I feel sad that he never had that experience. Zoltán was always inviting me and guaranteeing my safety, but this still sounded dangerous to me, given the history of his earlier predictions.

Then, in 1986, I was traveling in Europe with my friends Bob and Becky Spitzer. In Vienna, they suggested that we visit Budapest, which was only four hours away by car. I was afraid, but going with them felt safe. And Bob was open to turning back at any time.

This was an important experience. Crossing the border in the early evening, everything changed. It was the same highway I had walked twice in terrible fear. As the road grew dark, memories flooded back. We stopped for dinner, and I felt deeply moved to hear the waiter speaking Hungarian. In spite of everything, the language and the music triggered a feeling of being connected that I was not aware of until then.

I enjoyed our three days in Budapest, and I especially appreciated going with these friends. I learned that I was safe, and I loved sharing the beauty of the city and the special food with them. Zoltán was no longer alive, but we spent time with Edith. Since then, I've been back many times. Lots of my returns were with friends, including Linda and Eva.

Edith
1988

One of the highlights of my life was when Ben and Jock went with me to Hungary. They had always talked about going along someday. I love traveling with them, and I learned a lot about their relationship, in which they practice what they teach. Sharing my memories and feelings with them in Budapest was an important step in my healing process of letting go of resentments from the past that had clung to me.

Given my passion for connecting people whom I love and respect, I enjoyed connecting László with my friends. They love him and his paintings, and Ben and Jock acquired some of his beautiful works during our trip to Budapest. These now hang in their center on Gabriola.

I admire László tremendously. During the war, he helped people and stayed true to his principles. Later, under communism, he consistently turned down work for the government. Even when offered leadership roles in the arts and at museums, he refused. He married a Hungarian writer and now has a daughter and three grandchildren.

László with some of his paintings
1998

Even though our lives diverged and we did not see each other for twenty-three years, when we reconnected in 1989, it was as though we'd parted just the day before. Still creating beautiful paintings, he has never stopped being himself. Today, he is the most respected and celebrated artist in Hungary. For his ninetieth birthday, in 1999, the government honored him with its greatest award to a living artist. I was there to celebrate. In his honor, an exhibition of his paintings was held at a museum that, until then, had displayed only paintings of deceased artists.

László and I share our thoughts, experiences, feelings, and friends. Many of his paintings hang in my house and in the homes of friends who met him when we went to Budapest together. Andy and his wife Karen also met him recently, and they had a wonderful time together. They had dinner in an old restaurant with gypsy music, and László was singing happily. He and I see each other often, whenever I visit Budapest, and our bond is ever lasting. As with my soulmate Steven, time and distance do not matter in this true friendship.

Each time I go to Budapest, I also enjoy being a tourist, taking in the theater, the arts, the music, and the beauty of the city. I enjoy speaking Hungarian with Andy and people in Budapest. I love showing everything to my friends and I'm beginning to reconnect with the parts of my past that I like. Although I'll never be able to forgive some of what happened, I am nonetheless able to accept what was, including events during the war. I am at peace with my Hungarian background, but never again would I want to live in Hungary. I am grateful and deeply appreciative of living and having my family in Canada.

Meanwhile, in the spring of 1988, Virginia went to the Soviet Union and was delighted with her accomplishments there. In the 1980s, working for peace was her main objective, and she worked toward peace on many levels as she spent most of her time traveling all around the world. She never took vacations, other than a day here or there after a workshop. She used to say she owed herself over 6,000 days of holiday time. Margaret Mead once said: "Change has always come about by actions of a few committed people." Even one person can make a difference. Virginia was one of those people, and she touched many of us.

In June, when she came to Winnipeg from Russia, I noticed that she had difficulty with her digestion. Blaming it on the heavy Russian food, she didn't want to see a doctor. Her lecture at the University of Winnipeg turned out to be her last public appearance. In July, when we met in Colorado for the annual international workshop, she felt very tired. Soon after, she was diagnosed as having pancreatic cancer. She refused traditional medical treatment and spent the last two months of her life in her home.

Two weeks before she died, I spent a full day with her, and I'm grateful for that time together. Despite her very low energy, she was hopeful that she would live. She talked about taking care of herself in the future and living a hedonistic life. When I asked what that meant, she said she would take vacations—and that she'd have to look it up in the dictionary to see what else it meant. We talked all day, and she told me to take care of myself. "I did not take care of Virginia," she added. She took care of everyone else.

She also said that she was concerned that her ideas could become distorted, just as she had seen happen with other friends' teachings. I promised that *The Satir Model,* which was then being written, would reflect her ideas as she taught them. (It does, often verbatim.)

I was leaving early the next morning. Contrary to the previous day's experience of hope and plans for the future,

Virginia's last words when I said goodbye were: "I'll say hello to Paul." I cried all the way home. Her death on September 10, 1988 meant the loss of a great teacher, mentor, colleague, and friend. It also left me with a commitment to continue her work to the best of my abilities. This came naturally to me because we both loved our work and believed that people can choose to make their lives better. Somewhere, I know she is still doing important work. We are connected.

My own spiritual path has continued leading me to many wonderful people. A few years ago in Winnipeg, I met Marilyn Zwaig Rossner. A gifted medium since birth, she was giving an evening lecture workshop entitled "Messages from Spirit." She uses what she calls her "gifts of spirit" to communicate with those who have passed into the spirit world. I believe in life after death and reincarnation. Paul was, I think, a very old soul. I've probably had a lot of lives with him. From the moment our child was born, we had a special spiritual bonding.

In addition to being a dynamic and innovative speaker, educator, and therapist, Marilyn is the founder and dean of the International College of Spiritual and Psychic Sciences. This institute integrates science, spirituality, and universal human values. Its purpose is to promote interreligious and intercultural understanding for world peace, while having people remain true to their own faith and highest wisdom.

With her husband, John Rossner, Marilyn also founded the International Institute of Integral Human Sciences, for which she serves as vice president. This organization is affiliated with the United Nations for integrating science, spirituality, and universal human values in today's global village. She travels throughout the world teaching and healing.

That first evening, I was impressed with her vision, her authenticity, and her loving and caring for all people. She brought messages to some people I knew. Everything sounded both real and magical. Curious, I made an appointment for a private reading. The next day, we connected immediately. In the reading, she had messages from Paul that sounded like Paul. She also said that I should write a book. I said, "I do not write good English, and I already wrote one. I never want to do that again."

She wanted to know what I had written. I hesitated to say it was *The Satir Model*, thinking she would not know who Virginia was. But as soon as I mentioned the name Satir, everything changed. She jumped and said, "You knew Virginia?" We suddenly had a strong connection through her, and we've shared on many levels since then. Our relationship has developed into friendship and has opened new horizons for me. I am learning about the spirit world and beyond through Marilyn's close connection with it.

Jock, Marilyn, and Ben
2000

For twenty-six years, from their headquarters in Montreal, Marilyn and John have organized international spiritual science conferences. By attending these, I've met many special and wonderful people. I've also had the opportunity to present material as well as be a participant. Marilyn is now connected with my friends Ben and Jock, and many other friends and students. Through Marilyn, I am connected with Paul and Virginia.

My friendship with Marilyn and John enriches my life in many ways. She told me that I should not have any unfinished business with any people or any organizations because they would come back in my next life as family members. That concerned me. So, over the past few years, I've met and made peace with quite a few people I had totally dismissed in my life after I had problems or disappointments with them. I'm very aware that I've made many mistakes and done things I am not proud of. I also have regret for things I didn't do. I am proud of all my survivals and of what I did with myself during my life. As a person, however, I am not proud. I'm just stumbling through life and making a lot of mistakes. These are a learning experience, but I've never learned enough. I'm learning to be aware of my mistakes.

In her special loving way, Marilyn had a special birthday celebration for me in the middle of the conference in 2000. It was an unexpected event that meant a lot to me. Andy and Karen had their Jewish wedding at the same time, after Rabbi J. Gelberman's spontaneous offer to perform the ceremony on the spot. Andy and Karen had met in 1991, soon after Andy's separation from Carol. After his divorce, in November 1992, they married in a civil ceremony.

The Jewish wedding was an important symbolic event in our family's life. As mentioned, Paul and I had consciously decided to leave our Jewish background and our past behind us when we

*The family on Andy and Karen's wedding day
1992*

moved to Canada. We believed this would protect Andy and his future children from what we went through. We knew from experience what the consequences of being Jewish can be.

Andy didn't share Paul's and my background with his children or his first wife, Carol. When I talked about this with Paul, he used to say: "Andy is doing exactly what we taught him to do." Andy and Carol did not practice religion, so neither Steve nor Paul had any religious education.

Andy's second wife, Karen, is Jewish, and he did tell her about our background. Andy and I also decided to tell Paul and Steve after Steve turned eighteen. In the fall of 1998, we shared our whole story with them and with Carol. I felt relieved that everything was out in the open. I regret that Paul and I made that decision in the first place and that we stuck to it so long. I know—and understand—that people who did not go through what we experienced will never be able to understand.

As I've said, I believe that the past should not contaminate our present and future. That was exactly what Paul and I had set out to do. I tried to erase the past while building a new future. On the other hand, while I wanted to create safety from the outside, I created a prison on the inside. I always had courage, yet I locked myself into a position without freedom. I thought at the time that this was the best choice in terms of the safety and security we yearned for. Now, I recognize that I was paying a high price for my choice. I wish I had known then what I know now. In my heart, I always wanted to be free, honest, and open. This remains an issue for me, no matter how I may rationalize, explain, and justify it.

Meeting Marilyn reminded me of the first truly psychic person I'd met. In 1956 in Hungary, about four months before the revolution, I was at a party with a group of artists, writers, and painters. One of the artists told me that she was also an anthropologist, and that she lived in a museum.

This got me curious—how can a person live in a museum?—so I went to visit. In one of Budapest's major museums of modern art, she had a big room with a small couch next to a little stove in the corner. A huge sculpture stood in the middle, where she was working on it. She greeted me and then, still looking, said, "I'm very interested in your face, in your facial expressions."

I felt awkward and was glad when she turned away, asking, "Would you like some coffee?" I did. Once she'd served it, she said, "Let me see your hands. I read palms." Studying the lines on my hands, she told me I had a son and described Andy and Paul and our relationship. Then she added, "A year from now, you're going to be on the other side of the Atlantic Ocean."

In those days, we couldn't even dream about getting out of Hungary. There truly was an Iron Curtain. Nobody thought a revolution could happen. So I thought she was totally nuts. But I like nuts, so I asked what else she could tell me. And she proceeded to predict all sorts of things about Andy that later came true, such as his having two sons and being married twice. Years later, in Canada, I remembered this woman with amazement.

For many years now, the title and subject of my workshops has been "The Journey to Self." It's about discovering how we became who we are and getting in touch with our inner yearnings, a sense of self, and the resources to become the kind of people we want to be. It is a lifelong journey, in my view.

Finding out where we come from and where we want to go is a mystical, spiritual experience. All the techniques and approaches I've learned are irrelevant unless I connect with someone on a deep level and with compassion. When we connect with a person on a spiritual level, miracles can happen. This reminds me of another of my mentors, R. D. Laing. He was an artist in reaching people without prejudice on a soul-to-soul level. He connected with people on a deep level, soul to soul, without assumptions. Laing could feel and accept a person absolutely.

People can tell when this is happening. It's very difficult to explain or teach, however, because this is a process and not a technique. At the 1985 Evolution of Psychotherapy conference, Laing interviewed a young woman diagnosed as paranoid schizophrenic. In twenty minutes in front of an audience of more than a thousand people, this person had transformed into a secure, intelligent, humorous, and healthy individual. She felt connected to him, she felt understood, and she had developed trust in herself. He accepted her, and she empowered herself.

From him, I learned to respect, accept and to be curious with people who have serious psychiatric labels. I am fascinated to connect with people who have a different perception of the world from mine. This helped my work with psychiatric patients and now helps me to accept everybody on the human level of having unique world views rather than the level of having diagnostic labels.

I feel privileged to participate with people in their process of discovery. I become the compassionate observer, witness, and guide during their tragedies, successes, pains, and struggles. I witness their courage as well as the loving connections they live within. I believe that each individual is the complex total of his or her experiences, including those before birth. In addition, all the generations that came before us have an impact on who we become. We sometimes discover that we share characteristics of our grandparents and parents, that we continue some old and irrelevant family rules, that we still carry family secrets that everybody knows about anyway, or that we've learned patterns of behavior. We may not like those behaviors in others, yet we tend to repeat them ourselves. Like them or not, we learn and integrate these familiar ways of coping.

In the process of looking back, it's exciting to discover what people really felt and never shared with those in their families, and to uncover the silent and unspoken struggles of earlier generations. As we broaden our often-distorted perceptions and interpretations, we learn to appreciate the people who lived before us and to appreciate ourselves. Let's face it, all our memories and perceptions are our own interpretations, anyway. That's all we have. We cannot change events of the past, but we can change their impact on us. We can become our own decision- and choice-makers in the context of our present opportunities and dreams. We can let go of what no longer fits, transform what's no longer useful, and accept what cannot be changed. More and more, for better or worse, I realize how my present priorities, choices, and coping mechanisms reflect my earlier experiences and values. Whatever my experience in the here and now, it rings a bell with some memory of the past.

I'm also grateful to be healthy and free to live as I want. Those who know me know that I continue to live dangerously, in a way. At my age, I know I "should" slow down. Each year, I decide that I will. Yet, each year I get busier, travel more, give more workshops, and do more of everything that interests me. I recently read this quote: ""Do what you love and love what you are doing, and you will never work another day in your life."* This is certainly true for me. I love what I do, and I don't consider it work. Each person I meet is a puzzle and a gift.

My two priorities are my family and my work. My love for Andy and my grandsons is my biggest blessing. I want to share my learnings with them, have meals with them, and spend as much time with them as possible. We're very close, and we talk about everything. I enjoy my friendship with them, and I love them unconditionally. I want to give them whatever I can while I'm living. In the last minutes of my life, I don't want to think that I didn't spend enough time with the people who are closest to me.

What keeps me in Winnipeg is that both Andy and Paul live here. Many of my dearest friends live elsewhere, but that doesn't affect my love for them or our relationships. I'm grateful to have a few wonderful friends I can trust and feel close to. Looking back, I sometimes wonder how I got to meet all the special people I know or have known. I don't know how they came into my life, but I certainly noticed them. I think that's the significant thing. They continue to enrich my life, and I am grateful. People are very important for me.

---

* The Buddha, as quoted in *Chicken Soup for the Soul at Work*, p. 127.

There is a life beyond family and work, of course. I love movies, theater, music, books, ice cream, chocolate, and travel for fun. Whenever I'm in my beloved New York, I go to two or three plays a day, if I can. I also love my home, despite its chronic disorder. It's full of unfinished tasks and all my modern toys. I am fascinated by the new technical miracles, such as computers and videotape machines. The problem is that I have difficulty mastering them. A slow learner, I go from one disaster to the next. It takes time, and I am fortunate that my friends are patient about teaching me.

In my earlier life, I was yearning for freedom. I did not know about internal freedom, I just wanted to live in an environment that provided external liberty. The most important thing I have learned in the last twenty years—and continue to learn today—is to strive for freedom and harmony within myself. This is my challenge now.

In 2000, when I turned eighty, Ben and Jock threw a day-long birthday celebration for me. They invited my family, my friends, and many special people I've met over the years. With so many wonderful people, this was a loving, caring, and moving

Me with Andy on my birthday
2000

*Paul, Andy, and
Steve
2001*

experience that I'll never forget. I enjoyed every moment of this beautiful gift. The day was so enriching, fulfilling, and whole that I decided I don't need a funeral. Celebrating my life and the people I love was much better.

As I proceed into my eighties, I am more in touch with the reality that I won't always be around. I want to take care of things so Andy won't have to worry about them when I go. Like any sensible person, I have written a will, assigned power of attorney, made a living will to indicate that I don't want to stick around if I'm not having fun, and so forth.

I also considered what should happen to my body after I don't need it any more. Various choices each posed problems for me. Paul had thoughtfully provided a double niche for our ashes. His ashes already occupy half the niche, and the other half was awaiting mine. The only problem was, I am terrified of both fire and being buried in the earth. The more I thought about it, the less sure I was that I could go through with either cremation or burial.

One day in 2000 when I was visiting Paul's memorial site, it became clear that a third alternative might suit me better. I found that I could purchase a crypt—built in a wall, well above ground level—to house my casket.

Feeling quite cheered by having discovered this option (and having always loved shopping), I got Andy's help with selecting a cozy spot within the building, out of the wind and weather. To my disappointment, however, these sheltered crypts were already taken. I didn't want an outdoor crypt, as I certainly wasn't going to have my relatives freezing in a Winnipeg winter when they decided to pay me a visit. I insisted we look elsewhere.

For the rest of that day, Andy and I toured at least five more sites in other cemeteries. In the end, I decided that being near Paul still appealed to me most. I also liked it that his site was relatively nondenominational. My weather-based principles began to bend, allowing me to consider the outdoor sites near Paul and my mother.

A staff member showed us the last three available crypts. She assured me that all the details after my death would be taken care of. I felt good, knowing Andy would be freed of this. In a burst of relief, I bought the crypt for $5000. I also chose a tasteful and simple casket, knowing Andy might be more inclined to go for the top model in my honor if I left it up to him.

For a long time after, I never gave this issue another thought. The following winter, I visited my childhood friend Eva in New York. We shared our wishes about our final arrangements, and she was surprised to hear that I had chosen this expensive option. She said she wasn't at all afraid of fire and would rather spend the money while she was alive. I laughed," Yes, maybe I should sell the crypt and spend the $5000 going on a cruise with you to northern Europe!" We both found this a wonderful idea.

I became just as obsessed with getting rid of the crypt as I had been with finding it. I wanted to arrange for my cremation so I could have a good time first. When I got home, I phoned the cemetery and talked with a different staff member. I told her of my new decision and asked how I could sell the crypt. After a loud silence, she explained that crypts constitute a final sale. They are not returnable. I suggested that she might let prospective buyers know that this one was for sale. Another silence. A spark of interest showed only when she realized that I might now be persuaded to purchase a cremation.

Since I always follow a process, I decided to see how things worked out regarding the sale. If it sold before I died, I would be cremated and join Paul on the shelf. If it did not sell, I would be using the lovely gray casket I liked and hiding out in the $5000 crypt.

To my surprise, the funeral director called back an hour later. He was curious about my change of direction and repeated the policy of no exchanges/no returns. He was interested, however, in selling me a cremation. I asked, "What would I do with an empty crypt?" He must have seen that he wasn't going to sell a cremation unless he could come up with an alternative for me. We jockeyed back and forth for some time. Then I suggested that I might consider selling the crypt back to him at a modest loss to me. This deal is still in process.

Thinking about this set of decisions reminds me of how much I am a Gemini. I never can choose between options. If I find two

---

* *The Facts of Life* (jacket copy)

pairs of shoes I like, I often end up buying both. I am also aware that in a crisis, I would rather choose life over death—in short, the cruise over the crypt. As Paul often said, "We are here to give life to the years, not years to life."

———

In this stage of my journey, my major challenge is to let go, to detach myself from people and from things. This is very difficult. I think about it a lot these days, and I also procrastinate. The more I want to let go of people, the more I hold on to some of them. And when it comes to family, I can't imagine letting go at all.

I think the best way to deal with death is to live in a fully conscious, compassionate, and loving way. I am not afraid of death, only of a process of being disabled or having pain. I believe in life after death, and the more I learn about this, the more curious I am to find out what's next.

I believe that loving and relationship are the most important meanings in living. As R. D. Laing wrote: "Whether life is worth living depends for me on whether there is love in life. Without a sense of it, or even the memory of an hallucination of it, I think I would lose heart completely."*

Because of my life experiences, I have an absolute trust in a divine something higher than I am. I believe in a higher purpose and design for our being: to accept what is, to have faith in the process of our lives and what comes after, and to let the river flow.

In light of the World Trade Center disaster on September 11, 2001, my beliefs, forged during a lifetime of dangers, are again being tested. I want to believe as Marilyn believes that this time of testing can lead to an evolution of human consciousness, that our common humanity can connect us. I want to believe as Virginia did that we can create a peaceful world in which our differences enrich rather than separate us. However, when I see the way terrorist acts have tested worldwide security and produced fear, even in me, I struggle to maintain my hope and sense of freedom. I continue to travel and teach as much as before, aside from canceling one event soon after the tragedy. Just as I was taking freedom for granted, I feel I am again living dangerously. I worry about family and friends.

I have lived and written down my twentieth-century journey. I remain curious about how succeeding generations will live and write about the twenty-first.

Appendix

APPENDIX
Appreciations

Thinking "outside the box" is trendy these days. Maria Gomori, now past 80, has always refused to be "inside the box" in the first place. A rare being who has mastered the art of personal freedom, Maria is dedicated to teaching others to do the same. She faced death several times to maintain the freedom that was so vital to her and, in the process, she wove the threads of that freedom to cultivate an extraordinary inner strength to be her own person, with the capacity to embrace life with relish and acceptance.

Simply experiencing Maria in her day-to-day existence has been profoundly edifying to me in altering my perspective on life. Now, in my fifties, I have learned through her to honor my own journey, value the difficulties I have faced and welcome my circumstances with curiosity and a sense of adventure.

Friends and I have often lamented the absence of substantive women elders for ourselves (in our younger years and currently,) and for our children and grandchildren. The telling of her story reveals Maria to be a unique elder. She is a remarkable synthesis of her personal background, and the extraordinary breadth of knowledge about human nature that she has integrated by studying with luminaries in humanistic psychology. This, combined with her many years of counseling and teaching hundreds of people throughout the world to transform their lives for increased fulfillment, leaves no doubt about the depth of her wisdom.

And, being Maria, she is not a typical elder. Because she has no investment in maintaining an image or proving a point, the usual distance-creating awe and parental transference that is usually afforded an elder doesn't occur. When she works with people professionally, she offers herself openly, has a splendid sense of humor and remains spontaneous, direct and genuine. She sparkles when she is interested and nods off when she isn't.

She embodies self-responsibility. Although her life has been dangerous, dramatic and tragic at times, she doesn't carry her history as a burden. Maria doesn't identify herself as her story, however she relates it in a deeply personal way that fosters enrichment and inspiration for those that hear it.

I experience Maria as the most delightful compatriot. We travel together, work together, hang out together. The best of girlfriends, she is interested in men, likes to shop for sexy lingerie and pretty clothes and rings, rings, and more rings. A year ago, she did the quick-disappearing act to set me up with an attractive man, then waited up to find out the scoop on what happened. She is an earthy woman, vulnerable in her attractions. When we travel in foreign countries, she walks for literally miles and climbs up and down hundreds of steps so she doesn't miss a single sight or learning opportunity. When she sets her mind to something she is dauntless. She is constantly taking video and snapshots, many of which are missing the heads of people. She embodies the feminine in every sense of the word: accepting and supportive, fierce and protective. She gets passionately angry at times, then will just as easily burst into lighthearted, girlish laughter. She can grump and complain in grand style, she gets giddy on a martini or two. She hates to eat vegetables and thinks nothing of seeing at least two movies and a Broadway play in a single day when we are in New York City.

—*Linda Lee Nicholls, Ph.D., Dip.C.*
Trainer, therapist, friend

This is the fascinating true-life adventure story of a remarkable Canadian woman born in Budapest, Hungary in 1920 of Hungarian-Jewish parents, who has managed to turn the darkness in her life into light and reach out to help countless others to do the same.

Former Manitoba university professor and "doyen" of the Virginia Satir Institute, Dr. Maria Gomori is truly at 80 a rare survivor of the Nazi "long march of the Jews" out of Hungary, from which she miraculously escaped in order to rescue her infant son, Andy, now one of Canada's leading neurologists.

Escape from the Nazis was followed with capture by the invading Soviet armies, from which she also escaped. Both times, she remembers, her intuition saved her when she acted on an inexplicable impulse to survive in order to care for her child.

Maria's life story is that of a classical alchemist in the Jungian sense: one who has found the most difficult ingredients in life— impossible circumstances and relationships—and transmuted them into occasions for a greater grace than could have existed without them.

Since childhood and youth, she has been able to ignite sparks among the stubble in a barren field and establish meaningful relationships with a series of significant others in her life whose imparted gifts, virtues, and strengths have become the building blocks of her own soul.

Like Virginia Satir, whose successor she ultimately became, Maria Gomori firmly believes and teaches her students that unselfish, loving relationships with good and wise persons can heal and transform us more effectively than anything else in life.

From one who has passed through the Holocaust and other unimaginable challenges of the past century, this is indeed significant advice.

—*John Rossner, Ph.D., D.Litt.*
Professor of History of Religion & Letters,
President, IIIHS

Maria was likely born strong and fearless, whether she knew it early or not. But it took the terrible events of wartime Hungary, her repeated confrontations with disaster, and her own dauntless determination to survive for her to reach the freedom she so passionately sought. This is the story of an incredible life. It reads very much as I have heard this spellbinding storyteller recount it in the many years of our 25 years of close friendship and shared work together. These stories have always gripped Maria's friends, colleagues and students across many continents. I think it will grip those lucky enough now to be able to access it in print.

—*Eleanor Adaskin*
Ph.D, family therapist, and friend

Since attending Maria's first Hong Kong workshop in 1986, I have felt strongly connected to her. I still remember vividly my experience during the demonstration of "Five Freedoms." I was chosen as the star. In that demonstration, I felt desolate, tearful and in total darkness.

I came out from my ivory tower and really experienced the world. As the star of the "Parts Party," I moved towards more integration and learned to be the master of my "parts." In that workshop, I also learned to "put my foot down" and draw my boundaries more clearly.

We have laughed, cried and argued with each other, as in any close relationship. Yet, we respect and love each other in spite of, and perhaps, because of that. And we have lots of fun in the process. I feel very grateful to have met Maria in this life. Through her, I have learned to love my work as a workshop leader and translator. I have also been privileged to fullfill my vision of working with Chinese people by sharing my knowledge and helping my friends in our development of both the Hong Kong and Taiwan Satir centers.

My Chinese friends who have attended Maria's workshops often remark that she must have been Chinese in a past life. Many of them feel so connected to and understood by her, and there is a strong bond despite the difference in cultures. What impresses people even more is the amount of energy Maria has at the "young" age of 81.

Maria's work helps people in many cultures unearth the gold in themselves and initiate the changes they want to make in their lives.

—*Marie Lam, Ph.D.*
Trainer and translator
Hong Kong and Taiwan

I have attended both Level I and Level II of "Journey to Self" and my intention is to continue to attend as many as I can. I greatly appreciate Maria's warmth, caring, humor and skill as a leader. In the workshops she was constantly creating unique opportunities for participants to learn more about themselves. Furthermore, the stories she told about her own life experiences had a deep impact on me. I was willing to share deeply in what I judged to be a very open and positive environment. What was amazing for me was that in every Family Reconstruction that we did, there were huge learnings for me. I have become more aware during these workshops as to how much energy I have blocked in my life having expectations that were not met.

I continually remind myself of Maria's words, "Parents do the best they can with what they have." For me, with that phrase alone I am much more accepting of my parents' parenting and less judgmental about my own. I would highly recommend this workshop for anyone with a family!!!!

—*Sue Muirhead*
Participant

I have recently taken the "Journey to Self" I and II work-shops with Maria and find it hard to believe how meaningful they have been for me. I feel I have really integrated the learn-ings and have changed my life. I respond rather than react and I am much more in touch with my feelings and expectations than I have ever been. I like myself more and my relationship with my wife has never been better.

I have been doing personal growth work for the past 15 years and can say the work I have done with Maria is the most person-ally impacting of anything I have done. What a blessing.

—Ron

The relationship with my mother had been very painful. Since her death 11 years ago I have felt regret, deep sadness and a lingering sense of "not being good enough." The learning for me in "Journey to Self" was profound. I feel a lightness and know I always have choices. Now when I remember my mother I feel my own joy. Maria is a treasure.

—Sheila Metcalf
Workshop participant

In 1985 you [Maria] stayed in our home in Milwaukee while participating in the Milwaukee Marriage Encounter Spring Con-ference. One of the nights, as you, my husband, and I were sitting around in our pajamas, you suggested I go to Gabriola Island for an encounter with Virginia. I went, and it changed my life. Vir-ginia selected me for the full reconstruction and I've never been the same. I returned home with a broken ankle and plenty of time to think and then to act.

In 1985 I returned to college to finish my undergraduate degree. I followed that with my Masters in Counseling Psychol-ogy, then a two-year postgraduate training in systemic family therapy, and finally all the course work for my Ph.D. I am all but dissertation. I am a clinical member of AAMFT and have a private practice in Phoenix, AZ.

Maria, I think of you often because of the part you played in my life. If you hadn't encouraged me to spend that time with Virginia, and hadn't coached me to write to her requesting a reconstruction, I would never be enjoying my life this way. Thank you so very much.

Six years ago Bob and I took a vacation in Vancouver and on the Island. I took Bob over to Haven By The Sea to share a bit of the magic I experienced. Virginia is still there. It was so powerful. . . . I do hope you remember me, so you can appreciate how much you remain a part of my life.

—Sandee Confare
Workshop participant

My first experience with "Journey to Self" and Maria Gamori was in the summer of 2000. I was inspired by and impressed with both Maria's energy and wisdom and the respectful way she worked with participants. Although I was one of a group of 35 (and not one to do individual work in the program), the insights I gained from observing, taking part in others' Family Reconstructions and from a "homework" assignment were invaluable.

I left with the knowledge of how to include myself, a greater understanding of projection, and for the first time ever, experiencing a feeling of love for my sister.

In the fall, I attended Level II where I had the opportunity through my own sculpt and participating in family sculpting of others in the group to work through some long-standing family issues and to come to a place of acceptance of my parents as people, as well as a greater degree of self-acceptance and self-worth.

In January of 2001, I had the good fortune or good judgment to attend a second Level II. Although I had no idea what would be there for me so soon after the last one, I quickly became aware (with the assistance of members of a small group) that no matter how well my life was going, I have always had a sense of "waiting for the other shoe to drop." I was not always conscious of the fear.

As Maria worked with me, I realized it was almost like a cellular fear that has been part of the life of my great-grandmother, grandmother, mother and myself. It was pervasive and an intrinsic part of who I was.

I say "was" because during the week, Maria created a sculpt with me that dealt specifically with that issue and it was very impactful. Since then that irrational fear is much more apparent to me by it's absence.

I have had many opportunities to feel what it is like to be free of that fear in situations that in the past would have been anxiety-producing. One of the times that may seem insignificant to others, was around having my photograph taken. To me it was huge and for the first time in my life I have had photos taken and been present for them. There are also differences that I notice in relationships with my friends and family. Saying "no" is one of the things that is easier without the threat of imagined fears around what would happen if I didn't do whatever anyone wanted. Another bonus is that I have been spending one afternoon a week on creative projects that I haven't allowed myself to do in a long time.

Watching Maria work, I was impressed with her creativity; in the number of different ways she was able to work with the Satir model, specific to the varied situations of the group members. From what I have witnessed Maria is tireless, present, down-to-earth, a wonderful story teller and great wit.

—*Marilyn Farrell*
Workshop participant

Bibliography

ben Gurion, David (1996). As quoted in *Chicken Soup for the Surviving Soul*. Deerfield Beach, FL: Health Communications.

Bernhard, Yetta (1975). *How To Be Somebody*. Brookline, MA: BFI Publications.

Bethune, Mary Mcleod (10/8/98). As quoted in *Bits and Pieces*.

The Buddha (1996). As quoted in J. Canfield, M. V. Hansen, M. Rogerson, M. Rutte, and T. Claus, *Chicken Soup for the Soul at Work*, p. 127. Deerfield Beach, FL: Health Communications. *(Opening quote for the epilogue)*

Camus, Albert (2001). As quoted in Katharena Eiermann, Selected quotations, Realm of Existentialism website (http://members.aol.com/Katharena E/private/Philo/philo.html).

Canfield, Jack; Mark Victor Hansen; Patty Aubery; and Nancy Mitchell (1996). *Chicken Soup for the Surviving Soul*. Deerfield Beach, FL: Health Communications.

Castañeda, Carlos (7/15/99). As quoted in *Bits and Pieces*. *(First opening quote for chapter 2)*

———— (9/10/98). As quoted in *Bits and Pieces*. *(Second opening quote for chapter 2)*

Dunning, Lewis (5/20/99). As quoted in *Bits and Pieces*.

Einstein, Albert (12/31/98). As quoted in *Bits and Pieces*. *(Opening quote for the preface)*

———— (1982). *Freedom, Ideas, and Opinions*, p. 32. New York, NY: Crown Publishers. *(Opening quote for chapter 9)*

Eliot, T. S. (1996). As quoted in J. Canfield, M. V. Hansen, M. Rogerson, M. Rutte, and T. Claus, *Chicken Soup for the Soul at Work*, p. 127. Deerfield Beach, FL: Health Communications.

Emerson, Ralph Waldo (1996). As quoted in J. Canfield, M. V. Hansen, M. Rogerson, M. Rutte, and T. Claus, *Chicken Soup for the Soul at Work*, p. 251. Deerfield Beach, FL: Health Communications.

Epicurus (7/13/00). As quoted in *Bits and Pieces*.

Foley, Elizabeth (11/5/98). As quoted in *Bits and Pieces*.

Frank, Anne (1952). *The Diary of a Young Girl*. Garden City, NY: Doubleday.

Frankl, Viktor (1959, 1984). *Man's Search for Meaning*. Washington Square Press.

Haley, Jay (1973). *Uncommon Therapy: The Psychiatric Techniques of Milton Erickson*. New York: W. W. Norton.

Havel, Vaclav (2001). As quoted in Katharena Eiermann, Selected quotations, Realm of Existentialism web site (http://members.aol.com/Katharena E/private/Philo/ philo.html).

Kierkegaard, Soren (1996). As quoted in J. Canfield, M. V. Hansen, M. Rogerson, M. Rutte, and T. Claus, *Chicken Soup for the Soul at Work*, pp. 259 and 275. Deerfield Beach, FL: Health Communications. *(Opening quotes for chapters 5 and 10)*

Laing. R. D. (1976). *The Facts of Life*. New York: Pantheon Books.

———— (1970). *Knotss*. London: Tavistock Publications.

Loeschen, Sharon (1991). *The Secrets of Satir*, p. 43. Long Beach, CA: Event Horizon Press.

McKeen, Jock and Bennet Wong (1996). *The Relationship Garden*. British Columbia, Canada: PD Publishing/ Highnell Printing.

Neill, John R. (Ed.); Salvador Minuchin; and David P. Kniskern (Ed.) (1982). *From Psyche to System, The evolving Therapy of Carl Whitaker*. New York: Guilford Press.

Nin, Anaïs (6/17/99). As quoted in *Bits and Pieces*.

Roosevelt, Eleanor (1996). As quoted in *Chicken Soup for the Surviving Soul*, p. 32. Deerfield Beach, FL: Health Communications. *(Opening quote for chapter 3)*
———— (6/18/98). As quoted in *Bits and Pieces*.

Roosevelt, Franklin (5/25/99). As quoted in *Bits and Pieces*.

Rossner, John (1999). *The Priest and the Medium*. Montreal: International Institute of Integral Sciences.

Russell, Roberta with R. D. Laing (1992). *R. D. Laing and Me: Lessons in Love*. Lake Placid, NY: Hillgarth Press.

Sartre, Jean Paul (1964). *Nausea*, p. ix. New York, NY: New Directions Publishing.

Satir, Virginia (1988). *The New Peoplemaking*. Palo Alto, CA: Science and Behavior Books, Inc.
———— (1989). *Old Sayings I Just Made Up*. Palo Alto, CA: The Avanta Network. *(Opening quote for chapter 1)*
————. (1991). *Thoughts and Feelings*. Issaquah, WA: The Avanta Network. *(Opening quote for chapter 14)*

Schwartz, Morrie. *Morrie: In His Own Words*. New York: Walker Publishing, 1996.

Schweitzer, Albert (1996). As quoted in *Chicken Soup for the Surviving Soul*, p. 107. Deerfield Beach, FL: Health Communications.

Shain, Merle (12/31/98). As quoted in *Bits and Pieces*.

Shinn, George (9/9/99). As quoted in *Bits and Pieces*.

Szasz, Thomas (1990). *The Untamed Tongue*, p. 91. LaSalle, IL: Open Court Publishing.

Thoreau, Henry David (1996). As quoted in J. Canfield, M. V. Hansen, M. Rogerson, M. Rutte, and T. Claus, *Chicken Soup for the Soul at Work*, p. 303. Deerfield Beach, FL: Health Communications.

Wong, Bennet and Jock McKeen (1998). *The (New) Manual for Life*. British Columbia, Canada: PD Publishing.